Following in the Footsteps of the Four Famous Flannerys

www.fourflannerys.com

Also by John Mulligan

Dancing on the Waves (Collins Press 2004)

FOLLOWING IN THE FOOTSTEPS OF THE FOUR FAMOUS FLANNERYS

A Walk Across Ireland from Coast to Coast including the Royal Canal Way

JOHN MULLIGAN

Published January 2007 by
The Connaught Telegraph,
Elison Street,
Castlebar,
County Mayo,
Ireland.
© John Mulligan

Reprinted May 2007

British Library Cataloguing in Publication data:

Mulligan, John
Following in the Footsteps of the Four Famous Flannerys
1. Mulligan, John - Travel - Ireland – Royal Canal.
2. Trails - Ireland - Royal Canal.
3. Mining – New Zealand.
4. Irish Interest.
5. Royal Canal (Ireland) - Description and travel.

10-digit ISBN: 1-906017-00-X
13-digit ISBN: 978-1-906017-00-2

Printed in Ireland

Dedicated to the memory of Brian Donnelly.

"Never judge a man until you have walked a mile in his shoes"

— old Native American proverb

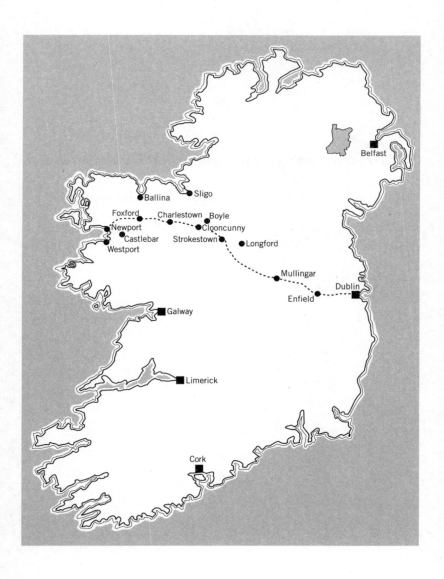

Contents

Acknowledgements

I would like to acknowledge the assistance of a number of people who helped bring this book from concept to reality. Brian Rogers first got me interested in the Royal Canal Way, and also helped by reading the text and making suggestions. John Breen read the first draft and his helpful advice has shaped the final form of the book. Mairie Cregan took the time to proof read the final drafts, and spotted several errors that would otherwise have slipped through. Ruth Delany, Ireland's foremost waterways historian, found time in her busy schedule to read the first draft and assist me with historical details; in addition, Ruth was kind enough to write the foreword for the book. The publishers made a generous gesture in forgoing all profits from this edition in favour of the Aurelia Trust, and Una Donnelly's kind sponsorship towards the printing costs has further boosted the percentage of the cover price that will go to this very worthwhile cause. Karen Carty and Terry Foley of Anu design have also been generous of their time and expertise, and the book is the better for their input. Joe McDermott proved a good companion on a long-distance walk and, as always, gave freely of his advice and help.

John Mulligan, October 2006

Foreword

In his last book *Dancing on the Waves* John Mulligan interspersed his account of a walk along the Grand Canal with thoughts about Romania's orphans, dedicating the proceeds of the book to the Aurelia Trust for its work among these children. In this his new book, describing his walk along the Royal Canal and on west to Clooncunny and to County Mayo, he uses the fact that he is walking in the footsteps of his four great grand uncles, the Flannerys, who had set out in the opposite direction to walk from their home in the west to Dublin to emigrate to New Zealand. He brings the reader with him on his journey, weaving descriptive and historical material with surmising what the experiences of the Flannerys might have been like.

The Royal Canal, which is to be fully restored to the Shannon in about two years, is both a delightful corridor ecologically and a waterway full of historical interest. Not only does the account of his walk encourage others to follow in his footsteps but also one actually begins to visualise the four young men making their way towards Dublin to board the emigrant ship. Having travelled across Ireland with him, in his closing chapters he brings us to New Zealand to trace the tracks of the Flannerys there, revealing an extraordinary story of grit and determination.

This book is an absorbing read throughout, and once again the proceeds will be dedicated to help the children of Romania.

Ruth Delany, September 2006.

Introduction

Sometimes when you go on a journey the thing you set out to find is not what you take home with you; instead you find a treasure that you never expected, something of much more value. This is why I like to put a bag on my back every now and then and go out into the countryside for several days on end, not only making a journey of exploration of the places I visit but also finding time for myself to think and reflect.

In the early 1860s four of my great grand uncles on my mother's side, the Flannery brothers, walked out their front door in Clooncunny in County Sligo and set out on a journey to Dublin. Ireland was still recovering from the great famine of 1845, and there was no future on a small farm for all the children of Tom and Una Flannery. The best hope of a future for these young men seemed to lie in New Zealand, and a passage was available on ships from Dublin and Liverpool. However there was no money in the Flannery household to pay for a train or passage boat fare to Dublin, so the Flannerys did the obvious thing under the circumstances; they put their few possessions on their backs and walked the 120 miles to Dublin to catch the ship to the unknown world that was New Zealand.

The Flannerys just wanted a few simple things in life. They wanted to get jobs that would give them a good living, and maybe enough to buy some land of their own on which to settle down and raise their families, away from the abject poverty and deprivation of nineteenth century Ireland. They found something more; a once in a lifetime chance to make it big in this new world of opportunity and promise that was so far removed from the world they had left behind.

I grew up with a vague awareness that many of my relations lived in this exotic land far away, a place that I imagined as some kind of land of milk and honey where everybody lived like kings on big sheep farms. When I finally got there, it was nothing like the land of my childhood imagination. I found instead a place that almost immediately began to feel like a home away from home, with a community of friends and relations that was as strong and as welcoming as the one I grew up among in Ireland. Clearly, the values of the home country were carried over the sea by the four Flannerys, and have stood the test of generations.

Over the years, some of the Flannerys drifted back. Not the original four of course, but their descendants and their own families. They came in ones and twos, on foot with backpacks, on bicycles, or in little rented cars. They stood blinking tearfully in the kitchen of the old house in Clooncunny, warming their hands on a hearth fire that had been kept kindled for several generations since the four young men had left. We filled them in on the stories of their missing relatives, the descendants of the ones who stayed behind. They brought stories with them too; stories of big men who played rugby for their province, who farmed the rich lands of the Ida Valley, people who had made their mark on all facets of society. I was particularly entranced by the stories they told about Brian Flannery and his three brothers, and the adventures they had experienced when they left this poor place in search of a better life.

Almost a hundred and fifty years after they left, I set out to follow in their footsteps. I wanted to see what it might be like to walk from Clooncunny to Dublin, although in my case I decided to walk the route in the opposite direction. I wanted to see what a walking trip of this length would be like, whether it would be a tough journey or an easy stroll. By walking it at a good pace I felt I would get closer to the four Flannerys; I might be able to understand better how they felt on the days immediately after they had left their small farm on the shore of Lough Gara. Just as the Flannerys found more than they expected when they left home, I found out a little more about myself and who I am, and I came back with a lot of respect for the four men who emigrated from Clooncunny; the four famous Flannery brothers. The story of their adventures is so extraordinary that it deserves to be told, and I hope that I have done justice to their memory and to their achievements. This book therefore is as much theirs as it is mine, and I hope you will enjoy it.

1

The Idea

The dew is falling on the hills
The stars are shining high
I hear the murmur of the rills
That sweep the heather by

John Keegan Casey. 1846–1870

Rowan Gillespie is one of my favourite sculptors; his witty and clever sculpture of a climber that seems to be striving to reach the top of the Treasury building in Dublin's Grand Canal Street has turned a mediocre office building into a landmark. Gillespie's most important work however has to be the amazing famine memorial on Dublin's North Wall.

On my way from work to catch the train one evening I walked down to the riverside to look at the sculpture, or rather "sculptures", since the work consists of a number of gaunt figures grouped in an area of paving across from the financial services buildings, close to the customhouse.

They were taller than I had expected. I had passed them several times in the car, but I never had an idea of the scale of the statues before this. Now, as I walked among them, I began to appreciate how well the sculptor had captured the essence of his subject.

The tall bronze figures face the harbour, seeming to have set their sights on a better world far away, with their backs turned on Ireland. Their hungry features, and threadbare clothes frozen forever in a casting that appears to flap around the almost skeletal forms, capture vividly the horror of Ireland's Holocaust, the Great Famine. The figures bear their few possessions in bundles, and one carries an emaciated child on his shoulders. A mean looking dog brings harries them from the side; the sculptor may have intended some symbolism in this smaller piece, but it certainly adds to the feeling of misery of the overall installation.

In contrast with the light good humour of Gillespie's work in "aspiration", his famine memorial has the power to chill the spirit, and serves as a stark reminder of the fact that we are the lucky ones, the ones that got away. Those of us who live in Ireland today are the survivors of the great famine.

The placing of this monument is very true to the past as well. This quay wall was the place where so many of our ancestors boarded the ships that took them away from the land of their birth. They left in hope of better times ahead, sure in the knowledge that they would never see their homes or families again. The journey of our emigrants then, and indeed for well more than a century after that, was very much a one-way street.

As I wandered among the statues, my mind on the famine, I noticed that I was not the only one having a look on that early summer evening. Two small boys were playing around the sculptures, and indeed one of them was trying his best to pry the small statue of the dog loose from the pavement. I quietly suggested to him that he should leave it alone, and I was somewhat surprised at the ferocity of his response.

"Is it your fuckin' thing, is it?" he said. He couldn't have been more than nine or ten years old.

His young friend chimed in his support. "Fuck off and leave him alone", he advised me.

"What are you going to do with it if you get it out of there?" I asked him.

"I'm goin' to fuck it in the bleedin' river" he said, his little baby face belying his very adult vocabulary.

"And then what?" I said, trying to see if I could get him to think this thing through.

"Then I'm goin' to fuck all them big things in the bleedin' river" he said with a confident swagger.

"Yeah", said his tiny sidekick defiantly, "we're goin' to fuck them all in the bleedin' river"

I decided to try another tack. "Do you know what they are?" I said to them.

"Of course we do", said the first boy.

"Tell me so", I said.

"No I'm not telling you, he said.

The second boy seemed to shift into schoolroom mode all of a sudden. He raised his hand as a child would in a classroom, "Sir, Sir, I know what they are", he said.

The first boy turned on him in surprise. "No you bleedin' don't", he said.

"I do so", he said, "They're for rememberin' the famine"

"Me bollix", said number one.

"Yes they are, aren't they sir?" he said.

I agreed; they made up a famine memorial. I thought I would try my luck and see if I could get a bit further with this. "What was the famine?" I asked them.

Number two, who had been playing second fiddle, now seemed to be top dog, his knowledge setting him for a while ahead of the other boy. "A whole lot of the Irish died from the hunger" he said.

"When did all his happen?" I asked him.

"Back in olden times" he said. "Years and years and years ago"

"And how could such a thing happen?" I probed.

There was a bit of head scratching, and then number one came to life again. Some small bit of half remembered information wormed its way to the top of his brain, and he smiled at the good of it. He had the knowledge; he was the main man again!

"The fuckin' Brits done it to us" he said triumphantly.

The two small boys ran away along the quays, shouting out their mantra again and again as they ran towards the bridge over the Royal Canal dock, "The fuckin' Brits done it to us."

I turned and walked away, towards Connolly Station and my train home.

I had been planning for some time to walk the banks of Ireland's Royal Canal, from Dublin's North Wall to the river Shannon at Cloondara. Having walked the Grand Canal the year before, on a four-day journey of exploration of some of Ireland's industrial heritage, and I was hungry for more. I had heard that the Royal Canal Way was if anything an even more attractive route, which passed through some of the most unspoiled scenery in Ireland, and I was anxious to be off and explore its banks.

Following my trip the previous year along the Grand Canal Way several of my friends mentioned that they would have liked to walk it with me if they had known I was going, and that I should let them know if I ever planned a trip like that again. Most of them probably meant what they said at the time, but in reality I knew they might not necessarily make it if I called them and asked them along this time. Also I wasn't sure that I wanted company on the trip, I have got to the stage in life where I value a few days alone, and I am quite content with my own company.

There was one person for whom I was quite willing to make an exception however; Joe McDermott is one of my oldest friends, and he makes a good travelling companion. Author, historian, mountaineer, teacher, and fond of a good walk, he brings an infectious enthusiasm to everything he does, and the world to him is a wonderful place full of new and interesting possibilities. You couldn't ask for a better companion on the road, I thought, and his company would shorten the road.

I gave Joe a call one April evening. "Do you want to go for a walk for a few days in June?" I asked him.

"Count me in," he said immediately.

We discussed the distances we would walk on each day; we were both agreed that twenty miles, more or less, was an achievable target. The only other thing we had to figure out was a start date that suited both of us.

I had been giving the whole trip a bit of thought. When you get to the point where the canal enters the river Shannon at Cloondara, you are a just a mile away from the bridge at Termonbarry, where the main road from Longford to the west of Ireland crosses the river into Connaught. Thirty miles north west of the bridge, between upper and lower Lough Gara in County Sligo, lies the small town-land of Clooncunny, the location of my ancestral home on my mother's side. I have a great affinity with this place, and I wanted to walk the extra thirty miles to finish the walk there, where my much-loved grandfather was born, and where he taught me to fish and enjoy the beauty of the place.

Joe was up for it. "I'll leave the planning of it to you" he said, "and I'll go along with your arrangements." That was what I wanted to hear; I already had the route roughly mapped out in my mind, and I knew more or less where I wanted to break each night; I didn't particularly want to walk to someone else's schedule. I bought all the relevant ordnance survey maps and started looking at the details, spending a few Saturdays driving to points along the route and checking out the lie of the land. Every weekend I could, I would pick a stretch of the canal and walk it for up to ten miles, then return the ten miles to my car. I was gradually getting fitter, shaking off the inactivity of winter, and feeling more awake and alive. The canal was exciting too, a new environment for me, and quite different from its sister, the Grand Canal, in many respects.

I spoke to Joe on and off over the following weeks, and he came to stay with us for a night in April. He had been giving it a bit of thought as well. Joe lives in Newport, in County Mayo on the west coast of Ireland, and he had figured that his home was just another sixty or so miles from Clooncunny. It would be a pity, he thought, to be two thirds of the way across Ireland and not walk the rest of the way. "At my age, I might never get the chance again", he said wryly. The more I thought about his proposal, the more I liked it. As we talked, we brought the scheme a bit farther; there is no real practical walking route from coast to coast in Ireland, why shouldn't we establish one, just for our own interest? We could work out an attractive and safe route from Dublin to Newport, from the Irish Sea to the Atlantic Ocean, and it would give pleasure and challenge to anyone who might care to follow in our tracks.

A few days later I wandered down to the North Wall in Dublin to look at Rowan Gillespie's masterpiece, the famine memorial. When I turned to leave I saw the lifting bridge across the canal dock, and I realised that the canal finished almost beside the sculpture. The route we would walk would be a reverse of the journey taken by many of Ireland's famine victims as they abandoned their country in the face of starvation and despair. In some way, it would be our own personal tribute to the memory of the people who died and emigrated due to the famine. Anyone who cared to follow our track in the future would at least think about these victims, and their memory would be kept alive in a way that physical memorials could never achieve. Eight or nine days on the road would give walkers plenty of time for reflection.

The route we proposed to take would also pass by the door of the famine museum in Strokestown, located in the former home of the local landlords, the Packenham-Mahons. A local man bought the old house and estate in Strokestown in recent times, and he developed a well-regarded famine museum in the house, telling the story of Ireland's great hunger. The museum is an essential destination for anyone who wants to know more about this turbulent period in Ireland's history. We would also pass by the famine graveyard at Tempall Maol in County Mayo, one of many such places that contain the remains of hundreds of famine victims.

There was the other issue too; I had my own, more personal reason for walking this route. The Royal Canal was the motorway of its day – one of the busiest thoroughfares in the country, linking the impoverished west of Ireland with the commerce of the docks and the markets in Dublin. Many of the people fleeing starvation and poverty in Connaught would have walked this route on their way to catch the emigrant ships on the North Wall. The better off ones, I knew, had taken the horse-drawn "long cars" or the passage boats along the canal, but a lot of them, including the four Flannerys, had walked all the way.

2

North Wall to Phibsboro

The auld triangle
Went jingle jangle
All along the banks of the Royal Canal

Brendan Behan (1923–1964)

He was going to be late. I had taken a couple of hours off work on the Friday evening so that we could make a start on the first ten or twelve miles of the walk. Joe was due to meet me at Maynooth railway station so that we could catch the commuter train to Connolly station in Dublin, and we intended to walk back to Leixlip, catching the train back from there to Maynooth to pick up our cars. I had the tickets, and the train was due in a few minutes, but there was no sign of Joe. He had sent me a text earlier letting me know that he had been delayed in traffic, but that he would make it in time.

The train pulled in to the station, but still no Joe. Just when I was resigned to catching the later train and finishing the day's walk in the dark, a dusty red Volkswagen slid around the corner and nosed into the last vacant space in the car park. Joe emerged on the run, a broad brimmed hat on his head and his boots unlaced, and we scrambled on to the train as the doors were closing.

The train rolled past the stops on the way to Dublin, parallel to the canal all the way. The railway company had built their line on land that belonged to the canal company, and in fact they even bought the canal company and its assets outright in order to do so. From the train we could see the towpath for most of the way, and I pointed out some of the features that I had noticed when commuting to and from work over the previous year or so.

We emerged from Connolly Station in the hot summer sunshine, pushing our way through the crowds of commuters trying to escape the city for the weekend. At the station exit we turned right on Amiens Street and headed for Newcomen Bridge on North Strand Road. This is as near as you can get to the beginning of the canal – the stretch between the lock just above the bridge at North Strand and the river Liffey runs through land belonging to Irish Rail, and is fenced off from the public. That stretch is tidal also, and looks dirty and uncared for when seen from the bridge. Newcomen Bridge was named in memory of Sir William Newcomen, a Member of Parliament who had supported the Act that allowed the setting up of the Royal Canal Company.

Joe mentioned that he had walked this street hundreds of times in the past. Brought up on a small farm in north County Dublin, he attended school here in the famous O'Connell's School, beside the canal, and he came to school by train every day, walking from the station along the street just as we were now doing.

We turned off North Strand Road on to the canal bank, and wished each other luck in getting at least to the other end of the canal at Cloondara. This area used to be very run down, but in recent years it had been tidied up and was now nicely paved, with good quality benches facing the canal. All the benches were in use too, with a few groups of heavily tattooed men drinking cans of beer, but although they looked a bit intimidating they were no threat to anyone, just enjoying the summer sunshine as we were ourselves.

The lock keeper's cottage on the far bank looked a bit out of place in a city setting; it had a very rural appearance with roses in its garden, and was in beautiful condition. Joe took a picture with his small digital camera, mentioning that he would be interested to see whether the style of this cottage with its arched façade would be continued with any of the other lock cottages along the way.

We walked on under Clarke Bridge, at Summerhill Parade, stopping to take a photo of Joe with his old school in the background. The great bulk of Croke Park, Ireland's massive GAA stadium, towered over us on this stretch, and the canal runs right alongside the back of the stands. The two ends of the pitch in Croke Park are known as the canal end and the railway end, and are known to everybody in Ireland by those names. Not everybody however would be aware of how close both the railway and canal come to the stadium – the facility has been built to within inches of both. Up in the stand a party of schoolchildren, obviously on a tour of the stadium, was trailing behind their guide; they seemed more interested in trying to spot fish in the canal below them than in the imposing concrete structure they were walking through.

At Clonliffe Bridge where Russell Street and Jones' Road crossed the canal, we disturbed a young couple that were lying on the bank. They were wrapped in an embrace and each of them was drinking from a can of beer, with a large carrier bag of beers beside them, and a load of empty cans strewn around. A strong smell of urine completed this romantic picture.

The canal bank was blocked beyond the bridge, because of construction work on a new apartment complex being built beside the bank. Typically in our Celtic Tiger economy, there was no notice of apology for the forced diversion, and no directions as to how to proceed. We both knew our way around here pretty well however, and a short diversion to the right and then left again quickly brought us to the busy Drumcondra Road. We jaywalked our way through the chaotic Friday evening traffic and got ourselves back on the eastern bank of the canal, heading north towards Phibsboro.

The wide bridge where we crossed the road is called Binns' Bridge, and its name gives a clue to the early history of the canal. Binns is unique in having a bridge named after him on both of Ireland's main canals, the Grand and the Royal. Originally he was a director of the Grand Canal, but due to some unrecorded dispute he left with some other directors and helped found the rival Royal Canal Company. His influence with the very wealthy Duke of Leinster was, it appeared, a key to the flow of finance for the new canal venture.

Looking to our right as we crossed the wide roadway, we could see the railway bridge, which we had crossed earlier, carrying the mainline train to and from Sligo above the traffic. This line, we knew, would join us soon and keep us company for the next few days. The bridge is known locally as Independent Bridge, because for as long as anyone can remember it carried an advertising hoarding for the Irish Independent. Now these hoardings are being removed on many of our railway bridges, allowing us to see the attractive ironwork for the first time.

We stepped across some chains and on to the smooth footpath along the canal bank. This area used to be a bit of a no-go zone, with a lot of anti social behaviour and a good chance of being intimidated or worse. Now however the authorities seem to have brought the place under control, and I remembered that a few years earlier the area had been landscaped and a contract put in place for grass cutting and litter removal. A lot of people were out and about, enjoying the warm afternoon sunshine. Two young people were sitting on the bench by the double lock, and families with young children were relaxing on the grass.

A monument to one of our most famous writers, Brendan Behan, sat unmolested on the bank. It consists of a bronze bench with a very lifelike likeness of the writer sprawled on it. It occurred to me that it was almost the same distance from the start of the canal as was a similar monument to Patrick Kavanagh on the Grand Canal; both monuments were placed about one and a half miles from the beginning of their respective canals. We debated whether this might have been a deliberate decision or just a coincidence.

The canal companies originally designed the waterways with wide "building-free" zones on both sides, and this is what allowed later generations to build roadways parallel to the banks, as happened along Dublin's Grand Canal. This open space was still evident here, and brought a great sense of the open air to this city location. Here and there, individual workshops and assorted other buildings had been allowed to develop over the years, but these were usually small in scale and the overall sense of space was still evident. The new development of apartments, which had forced our diversion from the footpath between the previous two bridges, was an unwelcome divergence from the good planning practices of almost two centuries before, and was effectively creating a dark canyon around this beautiful city waterway.

We could hear the whine of a circular saw from Spain's small furniture factory on the far bank, and I remarked that it was good to see that such an old established local business was still busy enough to be working late on a Friday evening. The path on that side was also in new condition, and the line of trees helped create a picture of beauty here in the heart of the city. Close to the lock a beautiful willow tree completed the scene, making us wonder how it had managed to survive in an area that had suffered its share of vandalism over the years.

Another double lock towered above us as we walked on, with water cascading over the lock gates. It was obvious that these must provide a high lift, as the footpath was steep for quite a bit as it passed the locks. The walls of Mountjoy jail ran along the far bank at this point, and the huge ventilation chimneys of the jail dominated the horizon. Joe had the camera out again, taking pictures of the jail and the skyline.

We had barely passed this double lock, when another double lock forced us uphill again almost immediately; the canal rises almost a hundred feet in the first two miles out of the city, then steps up at a more reasonable rate before levelling out on a couple of long levels across the midlands. Ireland is a flat country, very suitable for building canals, but the canal builders had to get up the hill to the flat sections before they could take advantage of the topography.

The canal we had followed for the last couple of miles was a later extension of the original route; the terminus had initially been at Broadstone, about three quarters of a mile away across the canal to our left. The early canal had turned here, along the northern boundary wall of the jail, but this branch was filled in around the mid nineteen fifties. There seems to be no hope of ever seeing this branch reopened, and if I was not mistaken I thought that another huge apartment block under construction on the far bank seemed to be built very close to the bed of the old canal. Unlike the far-seeing planners of old, our modern day experts had allowed this huge building to encroach right up to the canal bank, creating nothing less than the sense of being at the bottom of a large cliff. The path, I hoped, would at least survive when the hoardings are taken down, and not be absorbed into a private development of apartments.

One of the reasons why canals attracted public support in the early years, apart from their obvious value in opening up the country to trade, was because of their secondary use in bringing supplies of fresh water to an expanding city. The Royal Canal was no exception, and this now closed branch brought water to a basin or reservoir near Blessington Street. Through luck, or maybe an oversight, the closure and filling in of the canal did not affect the basin, which has survived to this day and looks likely now to be allowed to remain. It is known to the local population as "the secret lake", and can be reached through a small plain doorway in the wall along the park that replaced the now filled-in canal. Generations of locals have enjoyed the tranquil open space that the basin provides.

Ahead of us was Cross Guns Bridge, carrying the busy Phibsboro Road across the canal. This was formerly known as Westmoreland Bridge, having had its foundation stone laid by the Earl of Westmoreland in November of 1790. The double lock just above the bridge was also named in honour of the Earl, who was the Lord Lieutenant of the day. This was the first bridge to be built on the canal, and the ceremonies around its construction marked the start of the long and arduous process of getting the canal across the country to the Shannon. Had the early promoters of the canal known of the hardships and financial problems that they would encounter along the way, it is possible that they might have abandoned the venture there and then.

We paused for a moment at the bridge to have a drink of water and take stock of our surroundings. We had both spent time around here many years previously, and we knew the area well. I pointed out the building occupied by the carpet company across the road; this had once been the tram terminal for one of the Dublin tramlines, another efficient form of transport that had been allowed to die for lack of foresight. Whitworth Road ran parallel to the canal on our right, and the restaurant at its junction with Phibsboro Road used to be the Iona Garage. The Iona name was given to one of the first airlines to be set up in Ireland in the pioneer days of aviation; I recalled having read somewhere that the garage owner had had an interest in the venture.

The series of tall stone buildings on the far side of the road was originally the North City Mills, part of the industrial legacy of the canal. This was the site of a flourmill from the early days of the waterway, with the grain transported from the midlands by barge and milled here for the bakeries in the city. A detail that it lost on many people nowadays is that the original mill actually got its power from the canal water; the change in level at canal locks allowed some of the canal to be diverted through a water race that could be used to power mill wheels. Several mills of various kinds were set up along the canal at various locks, but they all suffered from water shortage problems in summer weather.

This mill was more successful, as the milling season for grain following the harvest coincided with a more plentiful supply of water in the canal. Eventually other more modern power sources replaced the mill wheel, and the milling carried on long after the demise of the waterway. We could both remember well the drama of the eventual closure, with sit-ins and protests going on for weeks if not months. Eventually the inevitable happened, and the doors were closed and the strikers folded their banners and went home.

Following the closure the newer office block to the front of the building became the headquarters of a security company, and some time later the old stone buildings were converted into apartments. I remembered my late friend Seamus Keeley telling me stories of the times when he went to the mill to repair the giant conveyor belts that carried the grain and the flour; he always reckoned that these stone buildings were so solidly built as to be almost bomb-proof. This must now provide some comfort to the new inhabitants, giving them a level of soundproofing which they would probably not get in the modern apartments that were under construction behind us.

When the four Flannerys got this far, they must have stopped to rest as we did, gazing in wonder at the noisy and busy metropolis spread out before them. This was the edge of the city at that time, and indeed the housing estates of Cabra and its environs are a relatively recent addition to this north city landscape. The four brothers must have felt a sense of excitement at what lay ahead of them; it was their first time to visit Dublin or any other city, and their experience of crowds up to this was confined to fair days in Monasteraden or in Ballaghadereen. Their feet must have been tired too; it was a long walk from Clooncunny to Dublin. Little did they know that their adventures were only beginning; indeed, like the canal builders, they might have turned and gone home there and then if they could have foreseen the hardships that lay ahead.

3

Phibsboro to Leixlip

Leafy-with-love banks and the green waters of the canal
Pouring redemption for me, that I do
The will of God, wallow in the habitual, the banal
Grow with nature again as before I grew.

Canal bank walk – Patrick Kavanagh 1904–1967

It was time to get moving, so we crossed Phibsboro Road and followed
the right hand bank down by the side of the old tram sheds. There
was no signpost for the Royal Canal Way, but we knew our way
around here and we guessed that the left bank was likely to bring us
to a dead end at some point.

Some new apartments had been squeezed in between the stone
buildings on the far bank, but there was no development at all on
our side. A low wall separated us from waste ground, part of the
land belonging to Irish Rail. The round tower at Glasnevin cemetery
was not far away to our right, "the dead centre of Dublin", as Joe
reminded me.

This section of the walk was through a part of the city that was
not the most pleasant, and I was glad of the security of Joe's company
for the next few miles. It is a shame that the authorities have allowed
these no-go areas to develop; everybody should be able to enjoy

these public spaces, but the police and others have effectively sur-
rendered control of many such areas to thugs and vandals. The large
tracts of unused railway land do not help either, and provide cover
for the young tearaways who practically control this area. The railway
company can do little about the problem either; they cannot dispose
of the land for development as it forms part of the reservation for
the proposed metro link to Dublin airport.

Like an oasis in the desert, the cluster of small and attractive
cottages by the bank on our side of the canal was a bit unexpected.
They were all in good condition and looked lived-in; it would be a
lovely place to live if it were not for the wasteland all around. Joe
surmised that these might be the so-called "coke-oven cottages",
named after the location of the Midland and Great Western railway
company's coke ovens which used to be situated nearby. I recalled an
estate agent being tied up and intimidated when he attempted to
sell one of these houses some years previously. The youths who had
been illegally grazing their ponies on the cottage garden had objected
to its being sold and their squatters' rights being upset.

As well as the canal, the railway dominates the landscape here.
The Sligo line, on which we had travelled earlier from Maynooth,
ran parallel to our course but had always been a short distance away
since we left North Strand. It would soon join us and remain with
us for several days; the railway company had bought the canal primarily because it provided a ready-made route out of the city for its
railroad. It was said that they had intended to drain the canal and
lay the track on the canal bed, but Parliament objected on the grounds
that closing the waterway would remove an element of competition
in the transport of goods, and they were obliged to lay the line alongside the canal.

Another line ran closer to the canal, in a deep cutting as far as
Binns' Bridge, then crossed under the canal and turned through Cabra
towards the railway tunnel under the Phoenix Park. The landscape
all around was one of abandoned sidings and the derelict remains of
railway buildings. There used to be a station close to here, which

opened in 1901 but closed nine years later, and the siding that once served the North City Mills is now no more and all traces of it have long gone.

We walked on, past the remains of bonfires and broken glass, crossing under the Sligo line by a very low pedestrian underpass. It would be a brave hiker who would walk alone here at night or even in late evening; the underpass was filthy and litter strewn, with the usual attendant graffiti. We could understand why the Royal Canal Way is not way-marked along this stretch; the markings begin further upstream at Ashtown. It is a pity; there is immense satisfaction to be had from completing the route of an entire waterway, and not being forced to miss out on part of the experience. If you travel all the way from the beginning to the end, you get a better understanding of the canal, from the point of view of its construction as well as its history and development.

The section of canal beyond the underpass was equally depressing, if not more so. The predominant feature of the landscape around here was the ubiquitous palisade fencing, often topped with barbed wire, with which factory owners attempted to keep vandals out of their premises. It didn't seem to be always effective either; many of the factory buildings carried the scars of graffiti and vandalism.

There is a series of ruined buildings, including a ruined water tower, as well as the remains of railway platforms and sidings just across the canal. This is all that remains of the old Liffey Junction station, which had two platforms and a series of sidings for shunting trains. It was a landmark on the journey to Dublin for us country people; as a child I could remember the excitement as the train slowed through the old station and rattled across the points. The station closed to passengers in 1926 and was closed completely in 1977.

The seventh lock raised the canal up again just beyond the railway crossover. The lock itself was in good condition, but was full of floating litter, creating an unsightly spectacle. The Sligo line was now close to us on the far bank, and the grim sight of Broome Bridge station came into view on that side, just below the bridge from which it gets its name. This station was only opened in 1990 as a commuter stop, and was built entirely from vandal resistant materials, with galvanised steel predominant. The local boys had other ideas however, and they regularly and systematically wreck the station that was put there entirely for their benefit and that of their neighbours. The place always looks terrible, and I knew from my regular commute along this line that ordinary decent commuters are very wary when exiting there, or indeed even travelling through this area. More than once, youngsters who ambush the trains from cover of the bushes here have subjected train passengers to stoning and intimidation.

Broome Bridge itself is interesting for a couple of reasons. It is best known for its association with the famous Dublin mathematician Sir William Rowan Hamilton. It is said that in October 1843, he discovered the "fundamental formula for quaternion multiplication" while passing either over or under the bridge, depending on whose story you believe. Neither of us was able to explain to the other what exactly was meant by quaternion multiplication, although we knew that it forms the basis for many software applications, but we took turns in taking each other's photographs beside the bridge where a plaque on the wall commemorates this important discovery.

Thought by many commentators to be perhaps the leading Irish scientist and mathematician of all time, Hamilton was Astronomer Royal, in charge of the observatory at Dunsink, where he lived until his death from an attack of gout in 1865.

This bridge is something of a Mecca for mathematicians, and attracts a gathering of interested members of the discipline once a year, when among other things they have been known to debate whether or not Sir William was crossing over or under the bridge when he had the flash of inspiration. It is often thought that he was heading towards the city from the observatory at Dunsink, a mile or so further on. Other theories suggest that he was out for a walk with his wife, and that he was crossing the bridge, but I go along with the first theory; he would not have come down from the roadway to scratch his discovery on the bridge wall along the canal bank otherwise.

Either way, this is a historic place and worthy of better than the graffiti and litter that it attracts nowadays. The vandals have even attempted to destroy the bridge by removing stones from below the arch, and by lighting fires under it.

It is a pity that the observatory at Dunsink, which survived through many decades when Ireland was a relatively poor county, now looks set to close for good. Vandals have already started to make their mark on the ancient building – they seem to smell opportunity when a building ceases to be maintained fully by its owners.

The other interesting feature of Broome Bridge is that it the first of the canal bridges to be doubled, that is to have an extra arch added to accommodate the railway line which runs alongside it. These double arched bridges are an attractive feature, and add to the unique charm of the Royal Canal. Their only disadvantage may be that they are probably too low to ever allow for the electrification of the line, except by lowering the track significantly. If this ever happens, I hope that the heritage value of these unique structures is recognised and preserved.

A short walk brought us to Reilly's Bridge, a single span over the canal where the railway crossed the road by a level crossing. We crossed the road and followed the footpath on the same side; we had been on the right bank of the canal since we left the road at Binns' Bridge in Drumcondra. The area ahead of us seemed better; we were gradually escaping the grim dereliction of the industrial and wasteland area of the past mile or so.

I had been concerned that the footpath might be blocked beyond the bridge; it had been closed off for the previous few months to allow for construction work along the canal bank. This stage of the work was now complete however, and a fine new tarmac footpath had been laid on the bank. A new development of apartments was being built on our right, near the water but not by any means as close as what we had seen previously. They were nicely designed as well, and the developers had taken a lot of extra care to produce a pleasing scheme of waterside homes. We both remarked however that it would take a brave person to buy a ground floor apartment here, so close to an area which had so many problems, but maybe the new development would help to clean up the area.

After the bridge, the surroundings began to take on a more rural appearance, with high hedgerows and tall trees predominant. The day was still hot but not too bad for walking, and we decided to push on as far as the next bridge before taking a break for a drink. We passed Ashtown station on our left, and we crossed over the canal at the bridge; the footpath was now on the other bank and would continue on that side for a few miles. The tenth lock, a double, raised the canal up again just beyond the bridge, and we sat for a while on the arm of the upper lock gate and drank some water.

The canal between here and the M50 motorway shares a very wide land reservation with the adjoining railway line, and but for the noise of the traffic in the near distance one could imagine that this was an isolated rural place. The area was lush and verdant, and we had the place to ourselves for the next mile or so. We soon passed the eleventh lock, another high double, and soon after that we reached the aqueduct across the busy motorway interchange, bringing an end for a while to the quiet section.

No matter how much you like the peace and quiet of the wooded canal corridor, it is impossible not to be impressed by the modern engineering work that carries the canal and railway high above this motorway junction. A new aqueduct and railway bridge had to be constructed, the whole project having to be carried out with as little disruption to the railway schedules as possible. The old Ranelagh Bridge across the canal stands unused, but it was good to see that it had been preserved and not demolished during the course of the work. Blanchardstown railway station was not so lucky; it had to be demolished in 1993 to allow for a temporary deviation of the line while the work across the motorway was going on. The station had lain unused since 1933, and was sited on the northern side of what is now the motorway.

Joe was in his element here, taking pictures from all angles with his digital camera. Eventually I dragged him away and we set off up the slope to cross the road at Talbot Bridge and pass the twelfth lock, another high double. This was once the site of a woollen mill, its machines powered by the falling canal water. A new hotel has been built here on the far bank in the recent past, and its terrace was crowded with customers, enjoying an open-air drink on this sunny Friday afternoon. A number of canal boats were moored here as well, including a couple of rented boats from a cruiser rental company in Thomastown, a place we hoped to get to on Sunday afternoon. This is really the closest that rented boats will go to Dublin, the canal from here to the city is not the safest of places for tourist cruisers.

On the other hand, we both agreed that we had now passed the worst of the rough areas, and that the walk from here on would be a lot more relaxed. Neither of us could be described as being easily intimidated, but it is nice to be able to stroll along without having to keep a weather eye out for trouble.

Castleknock railway station is situated just beside the towpath on our left, and the absence of vandalism was noticeable. There were the usual few small bits of graffiti, but nothing of any account. A tall security fence separates the station from the towpath, but incongruously, it terminates in an ordinary five bar gate; there would be no need for any intending trespasser to scale the high fence, he would just have to walk a bit further along and climb over or through the gate. We both wondered aloud at this; why did the designers of the station bother with the high and relatively ugly fence in the first place?

Within a couple of minutes the houses and signs of habitation had completely disappeared, and we were back in a lovely wooded area, with an abundance of vegetation and brambles all around. The pathway was down to effectively a single track, and we walked one behind the other along the next mile or so, Joe setting a fairly fast pace; he was fitter than me and was in flying form. Piles of empty beer cans were dumped here and there; this seems to be a problem in any quiet place near a big centre of population. We noticed that two chairs appeared to have been dumped across on the other bank of the canal, close to the water's edge, but as we got nearer we saw that they had been positioned carefully close to the back gate of a garden – obviously somebody's private fishing place.

The canal bends slightly to the left here, and at the same time the path begins to rise quite steeply, so that we were soon walking fairly high above the canal. As we turned the bend we were already about ten feet above the water, and we could see the path continue to rise ahead of us. The railway was still close by on the left, behind the bushes, and would be with us for quite a few days more.

This area of the canal is known as the "deep sinking", cut as it is through a hill of hard limestone. The canal company faced huge problems in delivering this piece of canal engineering, ignoring as they did advice to take a more northern route and avoid this hill altogether. Locking up over the hill was out of the question, as there was not a suitable supply of water to be had at the higher level, and the technology to pump water to the high section did not yet exist. The hard limestone proved very difficult to work, and needed an inordinate amount of hand drilling and gunpowder to force a way through. We could still see the marks of the drills here and there on the rock face on the far side of the canal, and it was very evident that the engineers had cut away only the minimum of rock to achieve a narrow channel for the boats.

The influence of the Duke of Leinster, who owned Carton House near Maynooth, was said to be the reason for this difficult route. He wanted the canal to pass the front gate of the Carton estate, his country residence, and to serve Maynooth, which was his local town. The extensive costs associated with the deep sinking and the Rye River crossing at Leixlip almost broke the canal company before it got properly started.

The deep sinking had its own peculiar operation methods when the canal came into use. Because the channel only allowed for the passage of one boat at a time, any boatman about to enter the section had to blow on an instrument like a huntsman's horn. If he did not hear an answering sound he was free to enter the cutting.

It was a dangerous place for boats too. A sudden stop by the boat, such as would be caused when an inattentive tiller man jammed the prow against the rock walls, could cause the towing horse to be jerked back and fall on top of the boat below. In 1845 one of the worst accidents in the canal's history took place here. A passage boat on the night run struck the rock wall and sank, with the loss of fifteen lives. The captain had given the helm to an inexperienced assistant while taking a break himself for some food, and the youngster managed to steer the fast-moving boat into the rocky wall of the canal.

Along here the path was not yet too high above the water, but still rising. The railway was above our heads at this stage; it was able to handle the grades to cross this hill. A nice cut-stone wall bounded the railway line, but it was covered in ivy and undergrowth and was barely visible. This whole area could do with a good clean up to make it more attractive to local walkers. The path is slippery and requires resurfacing, and the stone walls need to be exposed and cleaned up.

The railway was now about eight to ten feet above our heads, and the canal about fifteen feet below us. It was hard to believe that we were in the middle of the city still; there was a feeling of complete isolation here with nothing visible except the trees and bushes, and the ever-present ribbon of water on our right.

The path took another steep rise, almost up to the level of the railway, and also began to narrow still further. The canal builders had obviously hit very hard rock along here, and had cut away as little as they could get away with. We were now a dizzying thirty feet or so above the water. Amazingly there were a lot of bicycle tyre tracks in the dirt along the path; it would be very easy to skid on the slippery surface and fall over the unguarded edge into the canal below. Rescue of any such cyclist would be difficult as well; we could not see any easy way up or down these rock faces. It did not take much imagination to see how the accidents with the towing horses had happened in the past.

In spite of its shortcomings, this deep sinking is an incredible piece of engineering for its time. The construction of the Royal Canal commenced in 1789, before steam drills or mechanical excavators were invented; this section was cut from the solid rock by hand drilling with steel drills and sledgehammers, and by crude blasting techniques using black gunpowder.

There was still a bit of littering evident on the other side of the canal, although the heavy undergrowth had the effect of covering up most of it. Someone had gone to the trouble of uprooting the heavy street sign for Coolmine Road, along with its two supporting poles and their "roots" of concrete, and had carried the lot here to dump it in the canal. It must have weighed a couple of hundred pounds, so it would probably have taken two people to drag it all the way here.

The railway was about fifteen feet above the path now, and the water about thirty feet below us. The far bank seemed to be accessible from a housing estate on the bank above, and there was the usual heavy littering. At one point, a dozen shopping trolleys lay together, just out of the water. Some shopper would appear to bring their shopping trolley home from their trip to the supermarket each week, collecting a fresh one the following week.

Just before Coolmine Road we stopped to examine the drilling marks on the rock face on the far bank. The marks are very evident here; the work involved in drilling it by hand must have been phenomenal.

The path doesn't go under the bridge at Coolmine Road; you can see that the old towpath is still there, albeit overgrown, but it is not passable and there is a new path that rises steeply to the roadway beside Coolmine railway station. We carefully crossed the busy roadway and picked up the path, still on the southern side of the canal, on the other side of the road. The road where we crossed was the scene of the first-ever fatal accident on the Midland and Great Western Railway. In 1847 a railway employee was crushed when a locomotive struck the crossing gates, which had not been opened in time to allow the engine to pass through.

We set off down the steeply sloping path on the other side of the road, past the new sign for Coolmine Road. The canal is still in a deep cutting, and the channel if anything gets narrower and deeper along here, with the pathway about forty feet above the water at this point. The cutting here is along the side of a hill, with the bank on the far side being much lower down. We both wondered aloud why the canal builders had not switched the towpath to the far bank along here.

The surface of the pathway is cut from the rock as well, with outcrops of rock showing through a lot of the ground. As we walked along, the path began to drop slightly, imperceptibly, so that we gradually found ourselves getting closer to the surface of the water in the canal. A large new bridge loomed ahead, high above the canal and railway. At least nowadays there is an enlightened attitude to this kind of infrastructure among planners; in the past the canal was blocked and navigation limited by the erection of low-level bridges and culverts across the waterway. Unfortunately the smooth concrete surface of the new bridge and its attraction for graffitists set a discordant note. A high palisade fence around the bridge abutments has done nothing to deter the graffitists; they seem to be able to walk through any such obstacles. The path was still about ten to fifteen feet above the water as we passed under the new bridge, but the dizzying sense of depth of the deep sinking was absent.

A couple of hundred yards further on we came to the very attractive arch of Neville Bridge at Porterstown. This little bridge carries a narrow road across the canal – the railway crosses the road by a level crossing just south of the bridge. The bridge has been allowed to become very overgrown, and would merit a good clean up. Like the bridge at Coolmine Road, the towpath under the bridge is blocked and overgrown, and steep ramps have been built to bring pedestrians up to the level of the roadway and down again on the other side. In addition to the dense growth over the old towpath, it has been blocked off by the construction of a low stone wall just under the bridge, to what purpose we could not figure out. The Royal Canal Way switches banks at this point; we crossed the bridge and would follow the north bank from here to Ferran's Lock, some fifteen miles away.

A hundred yards or so past the bridge we scrambled up the steep bank to our right to examine an old partly ruined building that we had looked at from the train earlier. As far as I knew, this building had at some stage served as a school, but it seemed to relate to either the canal or the railway, being built as it was on the land reservation that carries both thoroughfares through this area. In an effort to deter vandalism, more ubiquitous palisade fencing had recently been erected around the building; maybe it will soon be restored to its undoubted former glory. It is a beautiful steeply gabled stone building and seems to cry out for restoration. We decided to stop here for a while and have some food and a drink.

I dug out the chicken sandwiches I had bought earlier in the railway station shop in Maynooth, and poured myself a welcome cup of tea from my thermos flask. I never walk without a flask of hot water for tea making; Joe on the other hand prefers to save on space and weight in his rucksack and only carries a water bottle, which he almost always manages to refill somewhere along the way. When he doesn't find a suitable water supply he reverts to plan B, he cadges some water from me.

We sat for about half an hour here in the still warm sunshine, eating and drinking and talking about life in general. Both of us had previously walked the route of Ireland's other notable man-made waterway, the Grand Canal, and we were agreed that so far the Royal Canal Way appeared to be the more attractive hike. Eventually, with an eye to the train timetable and our target of getting to Leixlip while the trains were still frequent, we reluctantly left this peaceful spot and headed back to the towpath. We stayed up on the high ground for about a hundred yards or so, before finding an easier route back down to the canal bank.

When we rejoined the path we noticed that someone had dumped a motorcycle in the canal by the far bank. This must have taken a lot of hard work, to manage to get on to the railway line and then manoeuvre the machine along the track for several hundred yards to get to this spot, finally heaving the bike into the water. Joe pointed out that in fact there was a second motorcycle dumped here also, partly covered by undergrowth. Maybe this is the dumping point of choice for a local motorcycle thief.

This is a lovely shady wooded area, with lots of trees, particularly ash and birch. The birch trees grow along the bank, which they obviously could not have done in the early days, as they would have made the towing of barges impossible. Now however they form a shady canopy over the waterway, their branches meeting overhead to create a leafy tunnel.

The wooded environs here, along with the wide strip of green belt that carries both the railway and the canal, gives a very rural feel to all this area. Although we were only a couple of hour's walk from the city centre, we had effectively left all of the built-up areas behind. This is in marked contrast to the Grand Canal, where it takes a good half day to "lose" the city on the way west.

The path bent slightly and brought us to Carhampton Bridge, beside Clonsilla railway station. The path runs up to the roadway here, but also runs through below the bridge. This is a very pretty bridge, ivy covered, and it was nice to be able to avoid crossing the busy road here. The station, although stark and modern, is nevertheless tidy and free from vandalism. It has one attractive feature, the significance of which can be easily missed. The stylish wrought iron footbridge over the tracks was originally located in Listowel station on the now closed north Kerry line, and was relocated here when the line closed instead of being broken up for scrap as was often the case in such instances – a little bit of railway history surviving in the middle of a commuter stop.

The wide grassy path stretched ahead into the distance, now down close to the level of the canal. The long straight stretch gave Joe a sudden turn of speed, and he was soon well ahead of me on the path. But for his occasional stopping to use his digital camera, he would have disappeared over the horizon.

We could hear traffic passing on the roadway to our right, but the road bent away to the north very soon after and silence descended on the canal once more. Up ahead was the hard outline of a large pipe crossing the canal, possibly a water main. On the far side of the canal we could see the thick woodland surrounding the ancestral home of the Shackleton family, they who gave us the famous polar explorer, Ernest Shackleton. Sadly the house is now out of the hands of the Shackleton family.

A good number of grey squirrels ran around on this part of the bank, or scuttled up trees as we approached. They seemed reasonably tame and unafraid of humans. These little animals have almost squeezed out the native red squirrel in most places. They are a threat to the native species not because of any kind of aggression, but because they are able to eat the nuts on which the red squirrels live at an earlier stage in the ripeness cycle, thus depriving the native species of their food supply.

A small set of steps to the right lead up to a narrow pathway, which takes you out to the roadway just where it bends away from the canal. This is one of these features that are often missed by passers-by; a few weeks later I tried to spot the path entrance from the roadway and was unable to do so at my first attempt; it is very much a secret for the locals and the walkers.

Beyond the water main and its attendant graffiti, the path and canal bent slightly to the left, and the whole area opened up. The closed-in feeling of the deep sinking was behind us now, and there was now a great sense of open space and fresh air all around. The buttresses of the old railway bridge loomed ahead; these used to carry the old Navan and Kingscourt railway across the canal at an angle and off to the northwest, before the inexperienced government of our young state dismantled much of our valuable infrastructure and opted instead to export our people for the next sixty years or more.

Joe waited for me at the bridge, busying himself with taking photographs of the stonework and the surroundings. We were both amazed at the condition of the old bridge buttresses; we agreed that it would take very little to reopen this crossing, just drop a bridge deck on the near perfect walls and you would be back in business. Other features, such as the cattle underpass leading to a nearby field, were still intact, and although the dense undergrowth along the original track bed hid the line from sight after a few yards, it would be a simple matter to implement a recent proposal to rein-state the line as far as Navan. In the current era of severe traffic delays and congestion it seems likely that this line must surely soon reopen.

The canal curved gently to the left as we left the railway bridge behind. The canal bank area was over a hundred yards wide in places; the canal company appeared to have acquired far more land here than was needed just to construct a simple waterway. With very little work, this space would now make a lovely public park for the people living close to here in the ever-expanding city.

On the far bank it was also apparent that a surplus of land had been acquired at the time of the construction of either the canal or the railway. A substantial plot of land separated the canal from the tracks over there. Joe surmised that this might have been acquired to allow for the railway junction that had developed where the lines had divided, but we could not be sure.

Pakenham Bridge was an attractive single arch span – the railway crossed the road by means of a level crossing some distance south of the bridge. Unfortunately a large cast iron valve on the water main that was clipped along the bridge wall obscured the beautifully carved stone nameplate of the bridge. We walked under the arch and looked at the bridge wall from the other side, but the water main people had been here too. Another water pipe was clipped along the bridge wall, and again the valve was placed precisely where it would obscure the name stone.

The area beyond the bridge boasts a wide flat grassy bank, and was popular with anglers, on this evening at least. Several groups of fishermen were either tending to their rods or were just setting up their tackle and chairs. There was a great air of "the weekend is here at last" about all of them; they were all in good humour and responded to our greetings.

The railway line is close to the far bank here; the recent addition of a second line as far as Maynooth has encroached closely on the bank, and the tracks an ballast are clearly visible for much of the next mile or so. As the growth returns to the banks following the engineering work, this stark view will be softened and camouflaged, but for the moment it strikes a slightly discordant note. The attractive view to the right is across open farmland, below the level of the canal which is now carried on a slight embankment, but this too will surely soon change as the city needs more land for housing. A wide section of the canal here was most likely excavated to form a turning circle for barges.

Around here you get the feeling of being out in the country, the city was now well behind us. The canal straightened out, with a long section stretching ahead as far as the eye could see. A good few people were fishing or just sunbathing and picnicking, but it was hot work carrying a rucksack and trying to keep up with Joe McDermott. Despite the relatively large numbers of people, the place was big enough to lose them all, and there was no sense of being in any kind of a crowded environment. I could see past him in the distance to where the canal made a slight right turn as it approached Collins Bridge, and I caught him just before the bridge as he photographed the remains of the old Coldblow railway station on the far bank. All that is left of this is the small waiting room on the platform beside the canal; the station buildings on the other side of the track have long been converted into a private house, and extended beyond all recognition. We talked a while about how useful this station would be nowadays, if the land here is ever developed for housing. The original station sat at the junction of the branch line to Lucan, but this line is now long gone.

It was clear that the more interesting parts of the canal were the more difficult to build, while conversely these more boring stretches would have been very simple and fast to construct. All that had to be done on the previous stretch would have been the excavation of the channel, with the excavated soil used to build the banks, nothing to carry in or nothing to carry away. With the exception of a few culverts below the canal bed to allow for the natural drainage of the farmland to the north, the last section could have been built very cheaply and quickly.

Another anomaly was also obvious to us along this section of canal. There were a good number of fishing markers spaced out along the bank, but the anglers who were out enjoying their fishing on this summer evening were without exception fishing from points which were unmarked. The markers too showed the history of responsibility for the maintenance of the canal; they were cast with the logo of the Office of Public Works, but the care of the canal has now passed to Waterways Ireland. It goes to show that nothing is permanent.

We walked on, following the towpath under Collins Bridge. The name stone on the bridge in this case was not obscured by the water main that was clipped to the bridge wall, but lichens obscured the name and made it difficult to read. We marvelled at the design and construction of this type of canal bridge. Built more than two hundred years before to cater for pedestrian and horse drawn traffic, it now carries a daily load of cars and trucks with no signs of weakening. The arch was almost flat in section, with only about four inches difference in level between the keystone and the four stones on either side of it. The structure looked as if it could not possibly support its own weight, but it has stood firm for all this time and seems set to stand for as long more again.

Past the bridge, the gently curving canal and its grassy banks made for a lovely walk. Off to our left we could see the Dublin and

Wicklow Mountains, and to our right was some nice level farmland. A few houses along here had back gardens that ran right to the canal bank, and most had small access gates on to the bank. Joe remarked that there must be very little crime or vandalism along here, if people felt confident enough to open their gardens on to the bank of the canal. One garden had a large double greenhouse, and although there were signs of one or two replaced glass panes, we were agreed that if it were situated a few miles east of here it would not survive so well.

The person who paced the fishing markers had got it right along here it seemed, and anglers were trying their luck at many of the markers after the bridge. This long level, from the 12th lock at Castleknock to the 13th lock at Deey Bridge near Maynooth, a total of around seven and a half miles in all, was the first section of the canal to be restored by voluntary effort in the nineteen seventies. As we walked along the gently curving section about half a mile farther on, a lazy left bend in the canal revealed the headquarters of the Royal Canal Amenity Group, the voluntary organization who's lobbying achieved so much with regards to having the canal restored. Their voluntary restoration work on this and other sections, as well as their constant pressure on politicians, effectively shamed the government into getting on with restoring the canals. The headquarters in a simple hay barn type structure, but it is neat and tidy with a slipway and mooring alongside it, as well as a picnic and barbecue area. The general public owes a great debt of thanks to the people who achieved all this; without them the canals would not have survived.

The roadway came close to the canal for a brief stretch where the amenity group headquarters stood, and then veered away again. The land between the road and the canal is made up of football pitches for Leixlip Confey GAA club, and a keenly fought out match was in progress as we passed. We stopped for a few minutes to have another drink and to watch the football, until Joe waved the train timetable at me and we set off again.

Ahead of us we could see the double arch span of Cope Bridge, one arch spanning the canal and the other the railway line that is now right alongside the waterway. Passing the bridge, we walked on past Confey railway station that stands just beyond it. This is a modern commuter stop which was opened in 1990, and which had to have its platform demolished again some years later to allow for the laying of the second track to Maynooth. The new platform is actually cantilevered out over the canal, and the station is quite bleak looking, although free from any vandalism as far as we could see. There is a big turning circle for barges just beyond the station, cut into the right bank, and with the footpath skirting around it. This used to be the site of a well-known fuel market, where turf dealers bought the cargoes from the barges arriving from the bogs of Longford and Westmeath.

Joe could smell the finish line for the day, at the next station at Louisa Bridge, and he was bounding along with a spring in his step. I decided not to try to keep pace with him, and that I would catch him at the station, so I just kept my own pace and enjoyed the walk. The day was cooling down now, and even with the low summer sun shining in our eyes it was a very pleasant evening to be out along the canal. Lots of walkers had the same idea, and were strolling along on the gravel footpath – we overtook several people along the next stretch.

The path was stony here, and obviously very well used, and ran straight for about four hundred yards, before swinging left to line up with the aqueduct across the Rye river. This aqueduct is one of the most notable features on the entire Royal Canal; it was needed as a result of the decision to follow this more southerly line, which brought the canal alongside the front gate of the Duke of Leinster's seat at Carton House. The aqueduct carries the canal more than 80 feet above the water level of the Rye River, which runs through a huge brick-built inverted arch far below the top of the embankment. The aqueduct took six years to construct, necessitating the excavation and relocation of more than a million tons of earth. Nowadays it is difficult to believe that this is anything but a natural feature in the landscape – such is its scale that it appears to have always been there. It is estimated that the cost of the aqueduct at today's rates would have been in excess of 100 million euro.

A thought occurred to me, had the canal engineers made this embankment wide enough to carry the railway as well as the canal, even though the railway had not been planned when it was built? Had they shown great foresight, or merely over-specified the original structure? Several months later I mentioned this to Ruth Delany, the ever-helpful expert on Ireland's waterways. Ruth was able to tell me that the railway company had in fact widened the embankment to allow for the laying of the track.

Joe was standing on the concrete spillway looking west towards the massive industrial complex of the Intel plant, when I caught up with him. We stood for a while checking out the various landmarks and remarking on the impressive scale of the entire aqueduct. We still had plenty of time before the next train, so we carried on along the path until we had passed over the Rye River, hidden from us by the thick hedges and undergrowth. A short detour to our right, just before Louisa bridge, brought us through a now derelict public park and down towards the bank of the river below.

This area was cleaned up and made accessible to everybody as a public park a few years previously, but now sadly the vandals have taken over and very few people go here any more. This is a pity, because this is a unique piece of heritage. Back in the 1790's, excavation work for the aqueduct uncovered a thermal spring at this spot, with water flowing from the ground at a constant 75 degrees. A spa was built around this source of warm water, and various medical benefits were attributed to "talking the waters" here. We could see the large bath, with its elegant flight of steps at each curved end, but it has fallen into disrepair and is filled with stagnant water and empty beer cans.

When the four Flannerys came through here they must have wondered at the crowds of grandly dressed people emerging from their elegant carriages to bathe in the spa. Nobody ever did things like that in Clooncunny, except maybe for the odd hardy soul who would swim in the lake in late summer when the water would not be quite as bitterly cold as usual. A lot of the people living around Lough Gara would not have been able to swim at all, and certainly communal bathing in a huge hot bath would not have been a feature of life in the west. The Flannerys would most likely have quickened their pace and kept going, knowing that the mighty metropolis of Dublin was now less than a day's walk away, and that the first part of their journey would soon be over.

We turned back and headed for Louisa Bridge, another double arch with a ramp in between which led us down to the railway station. A few minutes later the commuter train rattled alongside the platform, and took us back to Maynooth. We had walked just a little under 13 miles from Dublin, not a bad start for the first evening of our journey

4

Leixlip to Enfield

My weary hands are blistered from work in cold and heat
And oh to swing a scythe today thro' fields of Irish wheat
Had I the chance to wander back or own a king's abode
'Tis soon I'd see the hawthorn tree by the Old Bog Road

The Old Bog Road – Teresa Brayton 1868–1943

We headed straight to the Glenroyal Hotel as soon as the train deposited us in Maynooth. The evening was still warm, and we had decided to have a swim in the hotel pool to cool down and rest our tired limbs. Our plan almost came unstuck when an unhelpful receptionist in the leisure centre refused to honour a gift voucher that they had issued to me previously, and we only gained admission when Joe parted with a large entry fee. The cool water of the pool was refreshing, and soon we were soaking ourselves in the huge Jacuzzi and debating our dinner plans.

"A steak, and a pint", said Joe, "would replace the wear and tear on this old body". I had to agree, and we made our way to "The Roost", one of the large pubs on Maynooth's main street. A young woman from Cork brought us menus and fussed over us, and the steaks were beautifully cooked and came with loads of chips and onions, just what the doctor ordered! Our chatty waitress seemed to recognize that we were hungry, coaxing us to fit in some dessert, and we duly obliged. As soon as Joe had finished his beer, we retired to my home for an early night.

The following morning we breakfasted early and drove to Enfield; we intended to catch the train back to Louisa Bridge in Leixlip and walk to back Enfield, some 15 miles away, making for an easy day's walk. It was Saturday morning and the small station in Enfield was almost deserted, with nowhere open to buy a ticket, but we boarded the train anyway and resolved to pay on board. The journey was interesting, providing a high-speed preview of the walk that would face us later.

By the time we got to Louisa Bridge we had still not seen a ticket collector, and there was nobody around at that station either, so we emerged somewhat guiltily from the station and picked up the path where we had turned off it the evening before. The morning was fine, with very little cloud, and a nice day seemed to be on the cards. We took off our jackets and stuffed them in our rucksacks, a bit of exercise would keep us warm until the sun rose somewhat higher in the sky.

We noticed something unusual about Louisa Bridge. Although built in 1794, it seemed never to have been widened, and had what appeared to be the original stonework on both sides. Nonetheless, it was still wide enough to carry this main road, a thoroughfare which up to recently was the main route from Dublin to the west of Ireland. We wondered at this; if it was in fact widened at some stage, it was done with great sensitivity and respect for the original design.

The town of Leixlip has expanded a long way in recent years, and new housing estates now line the far bank of the canal, right up to the point half a mile on where the new motorway link road crosses the canal on a new bridge. A high voltage power line crackled and fizzed above our heads, bringing power to the sprawling Intel complex, which seemed to go on forever off to our right. The new bridge is called Collinstown Bridge 16A, and it was built in 2003. 16A refers to the fact that it is located between the 16th and 17th bridges; it would not have been feasible to rename them all to make way for the newcomer.

Past the bridge, a nice stone wall runs alongside the footpath, and a lot of giant trees, mostly chestnut and beech, line the walk. This area was once part of the out farms of the Duke of Leinster's estate, and a large stone-built house across the road from us almost certainly dates from the same era as the Carton Estate.

At the end of this stretch a small bridge spans the canal, and we could see the lower gate of a lock through the arch. This area is called Kilmacraddock, and the bridge, built in 1799, is called Deey Bridge. This was the first lock to be restored in 1977 by the Royal Canal Amenity Group, the voluntary body whose Trojan efforts helped save the canal for posterity. The lock was also the first we had encountered since we passed the one at Castleknock, 8 miles back on the previous afternoon; despite the extremely difficult terrain, the canal builders had managed to drive a level canal through a hill and over a wide river valley without using a single lock. They could not lock up over the hill near Castleknock, because of the lack of a water supply at that level; the canal here is fed primarily from Lough Owel near Mullingar, and in the early stages of the canal construction it was fed from the Rye River feeder at Ferran's Lock, beyond Kilcock.

The level crossing beside Deey Bridge is now automated, but up to just a few years ago a railway worker who lived in the cottage beside the bridge had to open and close the gates. I recalled that often at night you would have to walk across the railway; the crossing did not operate after hours. The cottage now seems to be closed up and abandoned; there was some talk of building another commuter station here but I don't know if that will ever happen.

We paused for a minute to admire the stonework on the lock walls. The attention to detail on what was essentially an industrial structure was amazing – the iron rope rings on the lock walls were set in circular recesses cut into the stonework, so that they hung flush with the surface of the walls. The craftsmanship was pleasing to the eye, and the work had withstood the intervening two hundred years very well.

A black and yellow steel barrier, with a narrow opening for walkers, prevented vehicular traffic on the towpath, and we squeezed through the gap and set off again. A new house on the right had a gate leading on to the bank, so it appeared that the owners had few security concerns in this rural place.

Canal, railway and roadway ran close together here, all at much the same level. On our right, a long gap in the shrubbery and hedges gave us a clear view across the road to the high stone wall surrounding the Carton Estate, and one of the attractive gate lodges could just be seen through the high iron gates. The Duke of Leinster had had the canal brought around here to pass by his front gate, half a mile farther on, and also to serve Maynooth, the village attached to his estate. At the time, Kilcock was actually the main market town for this area, but the Duke wanted to put his own village on the map.

Pike Bridge spans the canal and railway almost directly across from the main entrance to the Carton Estate. The harbour and wharf have been restored and cleaned up here, and vandal proof benches provided for the respite of strollers along the bank. This is one of the few locations from which the splendid Carton House can be clearly seen; the former home of the Duke of Leinster is one of the finest stately homes in Ireland. From here we could see the façade of the house and the lawn leading down to the "ha-ha" wall; landscapers of the time used this feature of a hidden wall below the surface of the lawn to make it appear as if the lawns stretched off to infinity across the grazing land beyond.

The former main gate of the Duke's residence is now the main entrance of Carton Golf Club. The house and the lands enclosed by the high stone wall have now become an up-market golf club, although the cheap garden shed being used as a security hut inside the main gate somewhat belied this fact.

The footpath from here on has been excavated to a depth of about four inches and filled with stones and gravel, making for a good dry walking surface in all weathers. This was done as part of a social employment scheme that greatly improved the canal environment for the residents of Maynooth, creating a pleasant linear park between here and the town. It is well used too, and we met lots of people out walking their dogs or just strolling in the morning sunshine, even at this relatively early hour.

The canal along here has more the appearance of a slow flowing river than an artificial feature in the landscape. It is amazing that something built for purely commercial reasons could have mellowed and improved in appearance to this extent over a couple of centuries. We debated that it was probably a different story around 1795 when this stretch was being excavated; a raw gash was made in the landscape and many people in the area probably resented the disruption to normal life caused by the work of the navvies at the time.

The tower cranes on the site of the new shopping centre in Maynooth had been visible on the horizon for some time now, making the town seem very close, but a further almost two miles and half an hour of walking were still ahead of us before we reached our first stopping point for the day. Eventually the new road bridge over the canal and railway at Maynooth loomed ahead, and soon our footsteps were echoing on the footpath under the wide arch. This bridge was built about ten years earlier to replace the old canal and railway bridges, in order to provide a wide access road into the fast developing town of Maynooth. The old railway bridge sadly did not survive the changes, but the original Mullen Bridge over the canal was spared and now stands alone and mostly unused beside the new double arched bridge. This new structure was built with more than a passing reference to its surroundings, and was faced with limestone to match in with the original architecture. A few decades of weathering will mean that this road-widening project will blend in quite well with the surroundings, unlike many such schemes that were carried out elsewhere.

The canal opens out beyond the bridge to form Maynooth harbour, a pleasant square of still water with a small island in its centre that provides safe nesting for wildfowl. The path skirts around the harbour, still on the northern bank, and runs through a small car park where the various cabins and containers of the social employment scheme are located. A few small benches have been provided on the western side of the harbour, set into the low wall by the footpath, and although most of them have been vandalised beyond use, one had a few slats left and we sat down for a drink of water and a short rest.

Across the canal we could see the new buildings of the commuter railway station, replacing the old station which closed to rail traffic in 1963, and which was reopened in the early 1980s. A shaky looking footbridge made from scaffolding has been in use as a temporary canal crossing for railway passengers for as long as I can remember, and we were both agreed that it was well overdue for replacing with a permanent structure.

This entire area has been reclaimed and laid out for amenity use over many years by a public-spirited group of local volunteers, but the selfless work they have done is not appreciated by a minority of local youths. The vandalism of the benches, along with discarded litter and empty beer cans, lend a dismal air to what should be a perfect location. The tell tale signs of nuisance crime were visible also; the sun reflected back from the patches of glass granules that marked the locations of several car break-ins. It is such a shame that a small minority set out to destroy the environment for everybody else; all the more remarkable is that this takes place just a stone's throw from the local police station.

After just a few minutes rest Joe was on his feet and anxious to be off; by the time I got myself organized he had gone around the corner and was almost out of sight. I caught up with him again before we crossed under the road at Bond Bridge.

The land on the far side of the canal was formerly an extensive area of sidings and loading banks for the railway in its heyday, but the ground has now been levelled and roughly surfaced to provide a "park and ride" facility for commuters. Maynooth has changed its status in recent years from a small market and university town to a large dormitory town for people who work in Dublin but prefer the quality of life in this part of north Kildare. The railway has had to change too; where it once dealt mostly in goods and cattle shipments, it now caters for the new customers with its frequent passenger service to and from Dublin. This has also provided a welcome bonus for lovers of the canal; anyone who wants to take a long walk in one direction on the canal bank can usually catch a train home, regardless of the time of day.

After Bond Bridge the high wall of the university runs beside the footpath for more than half a mile. Set up originally as a catholic university and seminary for the training of catholic priests, the college is now a fully-fledged university under the auspices of the National University of Ireland. It was built originally in 1795, at almost the same time as the canal, and the original arched opening in the walls can still be seen here. The college was allowed its own access to the footpath at this point, and the accounts of the canal company at the time show a small payment from the college for this privilege. This access was blocked up in the more recent past, probably we guessed in the 1960s from the style of the machine-cut limestone blocks used to close the opening. We debated whether the fee is still paid to the canal custodians, direct debited every year until some auditor queries the expense. We also wondered whether the opening had been blocked off to keep the young priests locked away in order to save them from the temptations of the outside world in the swinging sixties!

When the Flannery brothers passed this way, almost seventy years after the establishment was set up, the college would have been well established and the grounds and surroundings would have mellowed and matured. These young men would have had a lot of respect for this seat of learning. It was the sign of a prosperous farmer or merchant if they had a son in Maynooth; the reversed collar would guarantee not only status for the wearer but also for the family which had scrimped and saved to put him here. None of the four Flannerys would have even contemplated attending Maynooth; this was a place for people from another layer of society altogether.

We left the college wall behind after a while, and the road swung back closer to the canal on our right. This used to be the main road from Dublin to the west of Ireland, but the opening of the M4 motorway to the south of Maynooth has brought a modicum of peace to what is now just a local road.

About a mile from Bond Bridge we passed under the arch across the towpath at Jackson's Bridge. This is a spectacular piece of stonework; a multi-arched gem that crosses not only the towpath and canal but also the railway and an adjoining stream. It is a feature that many people miss; you could cross over it every day by road and not be aware of its appeal. The view of the bridge from the canal bank is very attractive however, and prompted Joe to dig out his digital camera again, giving me a chance to grab another drink of water. The day was warming up nicely now, and the sun was beginning to burn the top of my head, but as usual I had forgotten to pack a cap or some sun cream. I resolved to remedy this omission in Kilcock, now less than three miles distant.

The 14th lock stepped the canal and towpath up again just beyond Jackson's Bridge. We were now about 190 feet above the water level in the Liffey, but the rise had been almost imperceptible to us as we walked along. Apart from the small rises at each lock, the towpath is by its nature almost entirely flat along its length, making for easy walking, particularly over long distances.

The stonework on the 14th lock was of the same high standard that we had seen previously on other locks on this stretch. In particular, the manner in which the iron rope rings were recessed into the surface of the stonework was a charming piece of attention to detail.

The next bridge was a bit of a disappointment. The high and ugly slab of the accommodation bridge that is known as Bailey's Bridge has very little in the way of aesthetic value. It has obviously been reconstructed in the recent past, with differing levels of slab over the canal and the railway. We were unanimous that there was nothing we could hope for here in the way of improvement, except perhaps a demolition job, or at least some fast growing ivy.

The canal bent slightly to the right beyond the bridge, then ran straight ahead to the next bridge — Chamber's Bridge at the 15th lock. Before the bridge and to the right, between the main road and the footpath, North Kildare Rugby Club owns the land, and it was in good use on this Saturday morning with a lot of young teams training. Cricket seems to have a good following here also, with a number of young lads practicing their bowling and batting skills, and a cricket match was being played on one of the pitches. We stopped for a while here to watch the cricket; Joe was brought up in North County Dublin, and his home area has a long tradition associated with the game. Cricket has a reputation in many parts of Ireland as a game for the upper classes, but Joe remembers it as having solid grass-roots support in his home area, and he has retained an interest in it. To me however it is a game where a lot of people stand around the pitch for hours waiting for something to happen, and for once I was the first to move on and leave Joe following behind.

I waited for him at Chamber's Bridge. A short road leads from the main road to the bridge, stopping at the railway line. The road appeared to have been built just to access the lock and the lock-keeper's cottage, and the area is quiet and peaceful. A few fishermen were unloading their rods and associated paraphernalia from a car, and I wished them a good day with their sport.

Ten minutes past the bridge the road tapered in to join us from the right, running along the canal for the rest of the way into Kilcock. The footpath gave way to a wide and flat grassy bank along the roadside, and we hurried along this stretch; the constant passing traffic makes for a less pleasant walk than what we had been enjoying all morning, and we pushed on to get to the town.

The canal widens out in Kilcock to form a large harbour; this has been restored by local effort in recent years and is now a well-used amenity for fishing and all kinds of water sports. Its presence here close to a main road has also helped raise awareness of the amenity value of the canal.

The railway was still our constant companion on the far bank, and a train passed as we approached the harbour, the driver acknowledging my wave with a blast on the klaxon. The original railway station was located here but no trace of it now exists; it was moved westwards beyond the bridge and lock in the 1840s to deal with the problems that locomotive drivers had in starting westbound trains on the slight gradient. The relocated station closed again in recent years for lack of use, and when a commuter stop was required on the line in 1998 it was relocated again to a spot just east of the bridge. Not many railway stations get to move around quite so much.

We took a break for a cup of coffee and some cakes in a nice new café that looks on to the canal. It is a reflection of this town's new status as a relatively affluent commuter town that you can now get every kind of coffee imaginable in this once sleepy backwater. Kilcock is one of the best places for a rest stop on the whole route, with two very good cafés within a hundred yards of each other on the roadside across from the harbour.

I left Joe to sit and watch a group of canoeists doing some training while I walked to the chemist's shop to get a small tube of sun block. I joined him a few minutes later, and we set off again, passing the large double lock just above the bridge, and following the slightly winding towpath out of the town.

We could see the remains of the old Kilcock railway station on the far side of the canal. This was the second station, opened in 1850, and which closed again in 1963. At that time the town was in decline, and it was only in later years that its revival as a commuter town created the need for a new station, which we had passed a few minutes before just by the bridge.

At the time of the canal's construction, Kilcock was the more important market centre than its neighbour Maynooth. The original intention seemed to have been to bring the first phase of the canal directly to Kilcock, but the influence of the Duke of Leinster may have meant that the waterway diverted to Maynooth, at great additional cost. In 1796 in any case the canal opened for business as far as Kilcock, and the first boats began to ply their cargoes along the route. The passenger boats commenced service as well, although the efficient service provided by the fast moving "fly boats" did not come until much later. We remarked that Kilcock is one of those locations where transport plans have had to be revised again and again as the fortunes of the town ebbed and flowed.

The town is spreading slowly westwards, and new apartment developments lined the canal on our right, almost all the way to Allen Bridge, which carries the N4 road across the canal. This bridge has been widened in past decades, although rather crudely, but at least the navigation and towpath have not been restricted. A few more houses abut the canal bank just past the bridge, and then we were in open country once more, away from all habitation. The valley of the Rye River, the original canal feeder, lay ahead to the North, and the canal bent around to the left to head west parallel to the small river. At the bend, a spillway had been constructed to carry excess water back to the Rye, but today it was dry; the fine weather of recent weeks had kept water levels low.

Across the canal to the south, between the waterway and the N4, a large warehousing development was underway, obviously to take advantage of the new motorway intersection further west. It seemed strange to us, we were both agreed that this land would have been ideal for housing, being so close to a commuter stop on the rail line, but then planners seem to operate from a different agenda to most people!

The pathway here was grassy, but the grass was short and made for easy going. In fact, a cyclist on a mountain bike startled us as he raced between us at speed – we had not heard him approach from behind us. The land to our right was low lying and looked boggy along the line of the river, and the canal seemed to have been built along the very edge of the good land to the south.

Joe had been looking at the large scale ordnance survey map as he walked, and he told me that we were now crossing the border between County Kildare and County Meath, although there was no marker to suggest that this was the case.

Fifteen minutes later we arrived at McLoughlin Bridge, just before Ferran's Lock. Close to the bridge we noticed the stone-faced façade of the Rye River feeder, set into the bank beside the path. Tracing the feeder back down a small pathway, we saw the original sluice controlling the supply of water to the canal, but only a trickle of water was now flowing by it. The river itself was low also, and it was difficult to see how this small stream could have supplied most of the water for the early development of the canal, until it was eventually extended to Mullingar and could draw a substantial supply from the nearby Lough Owel. Yet this was almost certainly the main supply; there was no other water available at sufficient height to fill the waterway from here to Dublin.

The area around the bridge and lock is interesting and merit's a longer stop than we had planned on that day. Just past the bridge there are the remains of an old mill, complete with water race, but it was not clear to us whether the mill was powered from the canal water or from the Rye. I knew that at one stage an application to the canal company for permission to operate a cotton mill at this point was refused, due to problems with the water supply. The location of the old buildings seemed to suggest that the mill was subsequently fed from the river, but we could not be sure.

The railway crosses the road by level crossing at this point, with just the single arch of the bridge over the canal. There was a small railway station here in the early days of the railway, but this has now long disappeared, and the former railway cottage just south of the line is now a private dwelling.

We crossed the canal at the bridge to pick up the footpath on the south side. The pathway now ran almost alongside the railway, with frequent openings on to the track, and a train thundered by just feet away from us as we walked. The ground here was wet in places, and the soil type was more peaty and springy underfoot. This section of canal was built through Cappagh Bog, and was obviously laid out as close as possible to the good land to the south in order to take advantage of the firmer terrain, but in places it was clear that the banks were peaty. This must have been a nightmare for the builders of the canal; trying to stabilise the shifting and wet ground would have been difficult with the limited construction techniques of the time.

More than 200 years on, this is still an impressive achievement. Having overcome the almost impossible terrain of the initial stretch from Dublin to Maynooth, the engineers were obviously determined to avoid any further complications, and they strove to construct a canal at the lowest possible cost and with the highest possible efficiency in use. The stretch from McLoughlin Bridge just behind us to Thomastown Harbour more than 20 miles further on, was constructed without a single lock, and is now known as the long level. This is an amazing feat of surveying and engineering; the lack of locks meant that the canal was built more quickly and at lower cost, and also resulted in much faster journey times for canal traffic.

A turf industry developed in Cappagh Bog because of the excellent transport infrastructure of the time; it was rare to find a good bog this close to the city that could boast a canal running right beside it. In 1844 Charles Wye Williams built a factory just here on the south bank of the canal in order to process the turf using his new method. The moisture was squeezed from the turf by mechanical means, and the resultant product was moulded into bricks that were further dried and exported as fuel. Charles was a man ahead of his time; the process he invented was similar to the modern peat briquette system, but it was not a success for him and the factory closed again in 1849.

We passed the young man with the mountain bike a little farther on; he was lying on the bank with his shirt off, sunning himself, and he spoke to us in a cheerful manner in the accent which seemed to place him as being from Eastern Europe. Quite often, Joe remarked, some of our amenities are more appreciated by foreigners than by locals, who often take such places for granted and do not always make full use of them.

The canal bent around slightly to the left in a long sweep; it was not possible to see very far ahead on this stretch. The pathway remained grassy, alternating between the wet and boggy peaty sections and the drier patches of good soil. Eventually the large expanse of masonry that was Cloncurry Bridge loomed ahead, and we stopped on the bank just before the bridge to have a drink and a sandwich. We had walked about 14 miles since morning and hunger was beginning to bite.

Cloncurry Bridge seemed to epitomise what we had been discussing earlier, that the stone bridges built so long ago have the appearance of structures that almost defy gravity. The flat elliptical arches of these bridges seem as though they might collapse if a heavy load ever passed over them, but incredibly they have more than stood the test of time, now carrying heavy lorries on spans intended for horse drawn traffic. In this case however our concerns were to some extent justified; the bridge was the subject of a weight limit, and test strips had been set across some cracks in the masonry to monitor the subsidence.

The road that crosses the bridge links with the N4 half a mile away to the south. It is known as "the old bog road", made famous in song by local woman Teresa Brayton. This emigrant's song is still sung in foreign lands where Irish expatriates gather together.

We were reluctant to get moving again after our rest; we did not have too far to go and we sat for a while and talked about the journey so far. Something had been bothering me about the topography around Kilcock and I wondered whether Joe had been aware of the issue I had been puzzling about. The first phase of the canal, the history books tell us, opened to Kilcock and trade commenced on that stretch to Dublin in 1796. I was a bit puzzled by this; the valley of the Rye River was on our right as we walked through Kilcock, but the river appeared to run at a lower level than the canal. From where then, I wondered, did the first phase of the canal get its supply of water? I did not recall seeing any other feeder supplying the canal along our route this morning, so my theory was that the canal could not have opened for business until it had been excavated as far as Ferran's Lock, more than two miles further on. At the very least, the builders of the canal would have had to dig a water race from Ferran's Lock back to Kilcock to fill the waterway.

Joe thought about it for a minute, and agreed with me. Ever the historian, he figured that the answer could probably be found in the old records if I was willing to work a bit harder at the research. He opined that a water race could have been built along the subsequent route of the canal where we had walked west from Kilcock, and that the excavation of the later phase of the works would have obliterated all trace of such an original channel. To his credit, Joe never tires telling me that history can be very interesting, and at times like this I can see what he means.

There was no doubt however that just a couple of days walking by the canal had got me thinking about the way water has to be managed in order to construct a waterway such as the Royal Canal over a long distance. When the four Flannerys made their long trek to Dublin, their observations of the canal might explain some of the subsequent events in their story, when they faced a seemingly insurmountable task in the inhospitable Dunstan Mountains in New Zealand's Central Otago district.

"It's ironic", Joe said, "that the Flannerys left Clooncunny to walk to Dublin, and you are leaving Dublin to walk back. They would be very amused to know that you decided to walk with one of the descendants of the local gentry".

It was an interesting point. The Flannerys left post famine Ireland to escape poverty and misery in a country where the landlord classes lived off the fat of the land and the work of the tenant farmers. The local big house was called "Coolavin" and was inhabited by the McDermott family; now descendants of the Flannerys and the McDermotts were united in a journey of exploration on the road back to Clooncunny.

We crossed over to the north side of the canal again, following the minor road along the canal bank. Ten minutes later the road peeled off to our right, and we followed the canal bank again on the remaining mile or so to Enfield. The terrain was different here; the soil is sandy and firm underfoot. In fact, the canal builders had problems along this stretch, with the sandy sides continually slipping into the canal, and a lot of work had to be done to stabilise the banks here in the early days.

The old signal cabin of the Enfield railway station, with its large nameplate, soon came into view, and we could see the road bridge across the railway and canal in the distance. Enfield station used to be a busy junction, with a branch line following the canal westwards for a few miles and then branching off to Edenderry. The station is now only used as a commuter stop, but we could see that the old sidings just across the canal were in use to store materials for track-layng and line maintenance.

We walked up the sloping pathway to the roadway, and picked up the car from the railway station car park. Twenty minutes later we were back in Maynooth, turning the corner into the town car park at the back of "The Roost". Joe suddenly came alive. "A steak and a pint" he said, "would do the trick". I had to agree, and we headed for the upstairs bar and gave our order to the young woman from Cork. We followed the steaks with the obligatory apple pie; Joe leaned back and took a long draught from his pint. "Tell me more about the Flannerys", he said.

5

Enfield to Mullingar

There's music in my heart all day
I hear it late and early
It comes from fields are far away
The wind that shakes the barley

The Wind that Shakes the Barley —
Katharine Tynan 1861–1931

There is a bridge across the river that flows from Upper to Lower Lough Gara in County Sligo. Joseph Holmes owned a lot of the land around Clooncunny, the place by the bridge whose name means "the lawn of the firewood". The twenty-eight-acre piece that ran from the lake to the road was a sizeable enough farm for its time, and the hill was all good land. The Casey family were the tenants, and the farm was divided as part of a marriage settlement between the two Casey girls, Brigid and Una. A big ditch and a high bank were dug from the road to the lake in a straight line, dividing the small farm into two unequal halves. Nobody can now remember why it wasn't just split exactly down the middle; maybe there was an existing fence line there, or maybe it was divided on the basis of a bit of balancing to make up for some of the land not being as productive as the rest. Either way, the ditch and the old hawthorn hedge that now grows along the top of the bank form the only record that survives to mark what happened.

Brigid Casey married Michael Hannon, and Una (or Winifred as she was formally called) married a man who didn't have to come far to court her; Thomas Flannery lived just down the road in Lomcloon and he moved to Clooncunny when he married Una in the early part of the nineteenth century. They built a small cabin that was up a bit from the road but still sheltered from the wind that blew across the lake; later when they got on their feet they built a bigger house with three rooms down near the road. Tom and Una were my great great grandparents.

As far as I can ascertain, the young couple had nine living children. James grew up and joined the Royal Irish Constabulary, eventually becoming head constable, and he died in Athlone in 1920. John went to England, and may later have gone to America. I know that there was talk in recent years of someone from New Jersey who might have been descended from John, but the thread is lost.

Pat was born in 1846 as far as we can tell, in the middle of the famine years. He stayed home on the farm and married Biddy Sharkett from Ballinameen parish in 1876 when he was thirty years old; Pat and Biddy were my great-grandparents. Two years later their son Tom was born. Like his uncle James he also joined the RIC and rose to the rank of sergeant, in which role he served in Nenagh in County Tipperary. Sergeant Tom Flannery took early retirement from the RIC when Ireland achieved independence, eschewing the chance to join the Garda Siochana; he was my grandfather and my friend.

Pat's sister Nora was the wild one. The story goes that she fell in love with one of her first cousins from Lomcloon, and was run out of Clooncunny because of the scandal. The 1901 census lists one John Flannery aged 70 from Lomcloon with his wife Honoria aged 60. They had two unmarried daughters and one son living with them; Maggie was 24, Kate was 19 and James was 22; all of them could read and write, and the parents could speak both Irish and English. This must have been Nora's family, it seems likely that she married her cousin and lived out her life happily in exile from

Clooncunny, without having to move too far from the bridge.

There was another girl too according to family lore, but nobody can remember what her name was or where she got to. There was talk that she went to America too, that it was likely she was the oldest and went to America first, and that maybe she sent back the money to get the others their passages to England and New Zealand.

Tom was born in 1846, an "Irish twin" at a time when two children in a household would often be born in the same calendar year. Along with his older brothers Peter, Brian and Michael, Tom packed up his few belongings when he was only sixteen years old and walked to Dublin to make the long voyage to New Zealand.

None of the four who went to New Zealand ever came back. Tom married a young Galway girl, Ann Sammon, in New Zealand when he was 36 and she was just 22 years old. They sent two of their sons, Michael and Peter, back to Europe to fight in the First World War, but these two boys never made it home. Private Michael Flannery from the Otago Regiment was killed in February 1918 aged 30, and is buried in Tidworth military cemetery in England. Rifleman Peter Flannery of the New Zealand Rifle Brigade was killed four months earlier in October 1917 and is buried in Tyne Cot war cemetery in Belgium, below one of the twelve thousand white markers that run in precise straight lines in every direction as far as the eye can see.

The old house in Clooncunny is still there. The big ditch and the bank still run in a straight line to the lake, and the ancient thorn bushes along its length are tall and are ablaze with white blossoms every May. Paddy Flannery doesn't live in the house any more, but he didn't want to just pull it down either so he built his new house in the front garden and left the old house there for posterity; there was too much history in those old walls to just bulldoze it away.

Looking at this small farm now and the three-room house, it is easy to see why the four boys went to New Zealand. It would not have been possible for nine growing children and two adults to make a living off this piece of ground, and although the house was strong and dry and might have held all the children reasonably well, the place just was not nearly big enough for eleven adults. The only way up was to get out, and that is what they did. Family lore relates that they walked to the top of the hill and looked back just once at Clooncunny and the lake, and then never looked back again after that; the trip to New Zealand was a one-way journey in more ways than one.

We had sat up too late the night before, talking about my great grand uncles and their adventures, and the alarm clock interrupted my vivid dream of four young men walking along by the canal. Maybe it was the heavy meal I had eaten in the Roost that gave me such dreams, but I seemed to be walking behind them for miles, struggling to keep up with their long strides. I could not see their faces, just their backs in their long overcoats, with each one carrying a heavy bundle over his shoulder. I awoke slowly, for a while unsure of where I was, and turned off the alarm. It was eight o'clock, and I roused Joe and started to prepare breakfast. This would be my last night at home for several days; from now on we would stay wherever the day's walking brought us, and I needed to repack my rucksack with everything I needed for the next week.

Anne, my helpful neighbour, had agreed to drive us as far as Enfield on this bright sunny morning, and I gave her a call as soon as we had packed our bags. Anne is very tolerant of eccentricity, and made no comment at all at two middle aged men wanting to walk twenty five miles on a Sunday morning; she cheerfully dropped us in Enfield at the spot where we had left the canal the evening before. We stopped at the supermarket to stock up on snacks and water before setting off. As usual, I loaded up with a couple of litres of water; Joe was as ever happy to take the chance of filling his single water bottle along the way.

The footpath out of Enfield switches to the southern side of the canal at the bridge. On the far side the bank has been landscaped and is maintained as an attractive park by the people of the town.

Even at this early hour, a few people were out enjoying the amenity, bringing children to feed the ducks at the harbour just below the high bridge that carries the N4 bypass.

This stretch is very attractive, with a lot of tall trees, and the pathway is a drivable gravel road serving a couple of houses and the land further on. A ten-minute walk brought us to a gateway at the end of the roadway, leading on to the canal bank. An English fisherman was standing at his parked car by the gate, drinking from a mug of tea, and he cautioned us not to walk through the hot embers of his campfire. He appeared to have slept here overnight in his car to allow him to start his fishing early.

The railway had moved away from the canal bank as we left Enfield, but it was visible to the south, not too far away, on its own embankment. The canal was embanked here too, on our left, and clung to the slight hill on our right. It took advantage of the contours for a while, meandering slightly, with the ground dropping steeply to the south.

The fisherman we had met earlier was not the only one out trying his luck; a few others were camped along the bank for the next mile or so and were just setting up their tackle for the day. Fishermen are usually careful of the environment, but some of these were leaving a lot of litter and beer cans about the place, destroying the area that was at the same time giving them so much enjoyment.

A gate closed off the pathway where we passed the last of the fishermen, and we climbed over it and carried on along the bank. The grassy surface began to deteriorate; a local farmer obviously grazed his cattle on the bank and the ground was very cut up for the next half-mile or so. The canal was allowed to deteriorate for many years, being closed completely to navigation at one stage and effectively abandoned by the authorities; indeed it was only the actions of voluntary groups that saved the canal for future generations. Many farmers along the route habitually used the banks as grazing land, and there are still pockets where landowners have not accepted that the canal and its banks are public property.

The land to the left was falling away, with the canal clinging to the side of the hill on the other side. Gradually the far side also dropped, and the waterway was carried on an embankment to the point where it crossed over the Blackwater River on a stone aqueduct. An old stop-chamber just before the aqueduct would have been used to dam the canal in the case of a breach in the banks; it is now disused and its wooden gates have almost rotted away completely.

This part of the canal suffered a lot from deliberate damage to the banks in the early years of its history. Secret societies such as the Ribbonmen were active around here, particularly in the famine years of the early part of the 1800s. It was natural enough that many people, seeing food being exported by canal when the population was starving, would seek to slow down this trade. Breaching the canal would allow the water level to drop and cause the boats to run aground in isolated spots, making the cargoes easy pickings for these marauding bands. An additional spin-off benefit was that such vandalism also created work; quite often, it was said, a man who worked at night to cut the banks might get employment for weeks afterwards on the repair work. A small cut in the bank would allow the water to rush away, tearing away large sections of bank as it did so, with the resulting damage being greatly disproportionate to the efforts of the digger. A couple of hours of such destructive work by a very small number of men could create a month's work on repairs for a far greater number.

The canal company and the government did not take this disruption lying down. Squads of soldiers or often semi-private armies were posted to patrol the canal in vulnerable areas, and boats travelled together, often with guards, for safety. At certain times, all traffic on the canal was suspended after dark, with boats mooring together in secure areas until first light allowed them to proceed safely once more.

Apart from the general lack of prospects in the west of Ireland at the time, one of the reasons that the Flannerys left Clooncunny was said to be the rise in public disorder in the years following the famine. It would not have been easy for these young men to stay out of trouble at that time; many of the gangs adopted a view that anyone who was not one of them might be sympathetic to the landlord class, or, worse still, a police informer.

We stopped at the aqueduct to have a look at the structure. For some reason, the high quality masonry work that was a feature of the waterway so far was not evident here at this river crossing. The aqueduct has been repaired and strengthened in recent times, but it did not look as well built as the locks and bridges we had passed so far.

We carried on along the uneven bank for the next half mile, before arriving at the pretty Kilmore bridge, where a small road leads back to the nearby N4. Another fisherman was setting up here, surrounded by several boxes of tackle. I enjoy a bit of fishing myself, but new generations of fishermen seem to need a mountain of expensive gear in order to have a simple day out by a canal or riverbank.

The stretch after Kilmore Bridge is one of the most beautiful parts of the canal, or indeed of any of the Irish waterways, and it is one of my favourite places for a short walk of a summer evening. It is lined with tall trees; these had recently been pruned and tidied up, but without taking away from the overall vista. The railway had rejoined us on the far bank, and ran through the wooded area. On our side of the canal, the ground fell away to the north, the low ground below us seeming to have provided the material for the construction of the high embankment on which the canal is carried. Cattle had access to the bank along here also, and were damaging and eroding the bank with their hooves where they drank from the canal. It is a pity that the footpath along here is not kept secure from wandering animals, particularly given its popularity with walkers.

This pleasant stretch ends at Moyvalley Bridge, where the N4 crosses the canal again on its way west. All modes of transport to the west of Ireland meet here; the road, canal and railway coming together in what was an important junction in the old days. There was a railway station here for many years; the last remnants of the station disappeared with the widening of the road and the construction of the new road bridge in 1977. The same road works also resulted in the demolition of the ruined remains of the old hotel that had been established by the canal company at this spot. The hotel served for a while as a police barracks to deal with the activities of the gangs of Ribbonmen who created problems for the operators of the canal at various times before and during the great famine.

There was one house here beside the track where the owners had authority to operate a request stop for the train. Following the closure of the station, they could flag down the train if anyone wanted to go to Dublin. It is hard to imaging such an arrangement being made nowadays.

The N4 is very busy and dangerous here, with fast moving traffic making for a risky crossing for walkers. We decided to try to cross under the bridge in order to see if it was passable, although there is no footpath, just a narrow concrete ledge that was not quite above the level of the water. We walked along in the shallow water in single file, but the depth never exceeded a couple of inches and we got to the other side of the road without getting our feet wet.

Furey's pub by the side of the canal is a well-known landmark at this spot, popular with walkers, motorists and boaters. It was still closed at this early hour, and we were instead forced to shelter under the arch of the old canal bridge on the far bank when a very heavy shower made us run for cover. We took the opportunity of the enforced stop to have a drink of water and a snack, admiring the stonework of the old bridge and the way in which it had stood the test of time. In particular, we noticed an unusual feature of this bridge; the usual straight wall of the bridge abutment on either bank of the canal was made up of an arched structure in each case. In effect this bridge stood on four "legs", and we wondered whether it had been constructed in this manner in order to deal with bad ground. The method of construction appeared to consist of the provision of four solid foundations, one at each corner of the bridge. It might simply have been an experimental design that was not subsequently repeated, but either way it had lasted well; it was over two hundred years since these old stones had been laid.

The weather cleared and we moved on, crossing back to the north side of the canal from our temporary shelter. The route for the next mile or so is a wide gravel laneway and makes for fast progress. This stretch, close to the roadway and the pub, is a popular spot for mooring of boats, and an assortment of craft appear to almost permanently occupy the small number of moorings along here.

It was noticeable up to this that very few boats were to be seen on the canal at all. Apart from a couple of hired cruisers at Castleknock, and these few moored boats, the canal was almost empty of boat traffic. To some extent this is because the canal is not open for navigation over all of its length, but a substantial amount of it is now ready for use and the entire waterway will no doubt gradually get busier over the next few years.

We squeezed through a stile at the end of the laneway, moving on to a grassy bank with open fields to our right. The ribbon tail footbridge could be seen ahead in the distance; a simple structure with two masonry columns and an iron lattice deck, built, it is said, to facilitate churchgoers cut off by the canal. A pair of stop-gates, in perfect condition, is set into the stonework below the bridge. This long level had to be protected from breaches in the bank which would empty the entire section, hence this and the previous set of stop-gates. The presence of these stop-gates here and at the Blackwater aqueduct points to the problems with the Ribbonmen in the early years; indeed it is said that the footbridge is named after their activities.

I have often walked here in the past, and I am not quite sure of the historians' explanation that this was an accommodation bridge for churchgoers. My own view is based on my observations; a footbridge would have been necessary in order to operate the stop-gates, and would have been required when a damaged bank necessitated a rapid closure of the gates in order to prevent the canal from being drained and boats from being run aground.

I debated this with Joe as we walked westwards from the footbridge. He agreed that my theory was probably the most likely, but that there might have been some truth in the historians' version also. Possibly, he suggested, the bridge could have been built to deal with the damage caused by insurgence but dressed up to seem like a gift to the churchgoers.

The canal along here is raised on an embankment, with the land well below us on our right. It must have taken an army of men to raise this earthwork. The work was done in an era when the only motive power on civil engineering projects like this consisted of men, mules and wheelbarrows. The age of steam and mechanical excavators was still some way off; indeed if the investors in the canal had foreseen the way transport would go in a few short years, they would never have committed funds to the waterway. Unlike its sister canal, the Grand, this waterway was practically obsolete almost as soon as it was completed to the Shannon, and the railway age was just over the horizon when work was still going on here.

When the Flannerys passed this way the trains were already a feature of the landscape, although the canal was still the major carrier of goods along this route. Ireland was changing with the new infrastructure, moving slowly from a subsistence peasant economy to a trading one where goods and people could be moved around freely and relatively quickly. The boys could not have foreseen it at the time, but Ireland was opening up to trade and commerce and an eventual improvement in the living standards of its people. These improvements however were coming too late for these and thousands of other emigrants.

The Flannerys were big men, all of them six feet tall, with Brian standing six inches taller. Brian was the oldest and would have been the leader, making sure that they kept out of trouble and did not squander the hard earned money at the end of each week. They had left Ireland to better themselves, saving their money to secure their futures, maybe to get their own land one day and not be indebted to some landlord.

We could well see the damage that a few Ribbonmen might have caused along here. The canal on top of this high embankment, in a relatively isolated spot, could be attacked in minutes by a group of men with spades operating under the cover of darkness. A few channels to carry away the water, and the bank would be torn away in great chunks by the rushing torrent. A relatively recent breach, at the slight left hand bend before the harbour, had been well repaired and strengthened, but still looked fragile and vulnerable to deliberate damage.

The canal widened out to form a small harbour just before the aqueduct over the Boyne. This is known as Boyne Dock, and the remains of some canal side buildings are close by. There are two aqueducts here; the canal first crosses the Longwood road immediately after the harbour on a high single arched aqueduct, and a hundred or so yards further on it crosses the river Boyne on a magnificent three arched limestone structure, best viewed from the river bank below. Joe agreed to take my word on this – I had often taken the pathway that leads from the towpath down to the river bank, but we would not go down there today, in the interests of energy conservation.

A large diesel powered pump was operating down by the river-bank, delivering water up to the canal. It had been a dry summer, and the Waterways Ireland people were ensuring that the water levels were maintained in the canal for boaters. The canal custodians of old did not have access to giant diesel pumps, they had to manage water well in dry seasons, ensuring that only the minimum was lost when moving boats up or down through the locks.

We could see the railway viaduct just upriver of the aqueduct to the south. This entire area is a paradise for anyone interested in industrial history; the railway also crosses the Longwood road on a fine bridge, and a pleasant afternoon could be spent poking around here. For today however we would have to carry on; we had walked little more than six miles so far, with another nineteen miles ahead of us to Mullingar.

That was another thing. Joe was leaving the navigation to me, not too difficult a job, just follow the canal, but it meant that I was the one keeping track of how we were doing distance wise, as well as deciding how far to walk each day. I didn't want to put Joe off with the news that we were going to walk almost the length of a marathon before nightfall, so I had just told him that today's walk was "a bit more than twenty miles". No point in both of us thinking about the somewhat off-putting distance we were really going to face!

We set off once more along the trail, leaving the two aqueducts behind us, and the thumping sound of the pump gradually faded out and silence settled around us once more. This is a nice area with very little habitation, except for a cosy house close to the canal bank. The land was good, and much of it was given over to tillage, with a barley crop in one field rippling beautifully in the slight breeze. A sign nailed to a post in the hedge foretold some additional development; the landowner was seeking planning permission for a house in this attractive spot.

We were walking on a small roadway now, obviously the access way to the house we had just passed, but this road peeled away to the right half a mile farther on and we took to the fields again along the canal bank. This next stretch was very attractive, hilly and over-grown with a few sheep grazing here and there. The land seemed to have been excavated to create the canal banks, and had retained its random undulations, resulting in a piece of terrain which invited exploration at some other time. We were both agreed that this would make for a nice spot for a bit of fishing or a picnic; it was sheltered and something of a suntrap. The farmer here appeared to have spread his operations to the bank of the canal, and there was no definition between the public and private areas.

Another half mile brought us to Blackshade Bridge, and we squeezed through a style and crossed to pick up the route on the far side of the roadway. This is a very quiet road with little traffic, but the crossing point is well defined with a huge yellow warning sign on the path just before the bridge. Just across the nearby railway bridge on the roadway on the southern side of the canal there is an old cast iron sign of uncertain vintage, sadly now broken so that only half of it remains. The sign requests that drivers of heavy loco-motives should contact the chief engineer of the railway company before proceeding across the bridge; it was obviously put there in the early days of steam powered travel on the roads, and it is a miracle that it has survived for so long.

We headed on, following the grassy pathway on the northern side of the canal. This stretch was well fenced off, with the grass kept trimmed by Waterways Ireland crews, and we were able to make good time. We still had a mile to go to Hill of Down, where we planned to stop for lunch, and we were beginning to feel the need for some solid food.

This part of the canal is well sheltered by tall hedges and trees, and the far bank is heavily wooded right down to the water's edge. It is a popular location for anglers, many of whom camp out here at weekends in order to be able to fish all day. Sadly, some of these campers do not always take away their rubbish when they leave, and deposits of empty beer cans and food containers mar an otherwise very attractive area.

Rounding a slight bend, we could see a number of boats moored in the harbour at Hill of Down, and we soon passed through the style and on to the roadway. This is one of my favourite parts of the canal, and I often centre short walks around it, leaving my car in the yard of the café and boat hire company. Peter and Frances operate a small hire business for daily and hourly boat rentals, including an attractive narrow boat called "*the lily pad*". We sat down gratefully on the benches outside the small café, and Frances bustled about preparing a good lunch for us.

The railway had appeared again on the far bank, having emerged from the tall hedges that had hidden it from us for the past mile or so. There used to be a railway station here in the old days, officially known as Kinnegad and Ballivor, but the station closed in the early sixties, and now only a few ivy-covered ruined buildings remain just beyond the bridge. It is a bit of a puzzle sometimes that Ireland was much better served by public transport a century ago than it is today, although our present day national prosperity should mean that we would now have excellent transit systems, but that is progress I suppose.

Frances is a walker herself, and understands the appetite that can be worked up in the course of a nine-mile walk. She piled plates high with rashers, sausages and fried eggs, and brought separate helpings of chips and bread, along with pots of tea. Some extra large slices of her home made apple pie followed, and she filled my flask with hot water and topped up our drinking water bottles from the supply in her fridge. She only wanted to charge us ten euro in total, but we insisted that she take a bit more. I often have a feeling that this woman is reluctant to charge visitors to her café at all; she treats every passer-by as a guest rather than a mere customer. Being a walker herself, she has particular sympathy with other hikers. "I just wish I was going with you," she said as she wished us luck on our journey.

The sun was beating down hard as we took reluctant leave of this friendly place, and we stopped a little beyond the bridge to pack our heavier sweaters away in our rucksacks; it was tee shirt weather for the foreseeable future on this warm Sunday afternoon. The food had added speed to our feet and we very soon reached Ballasport Bridge, where the route crosses over the bridge to continue on the southern side of the canal. In the past I had missed the signs and walked the other bank, which is passable also, but today we decided to stick with the official route.

We had lost the railway somewhere after Hill of Down – it takes a more or less straight line across the boggy land to the south but the canal builders took the more winding route to follow the contours and avoid the bog. This stretch of canal, between here and D'Arcy's Bridge some three and a half miles away, runs through varied countryside. The land to the left is boggy, while the ground to the north beyond the canal is firmer; the canal builders hugged the good land as closely as they could, while maintaining a level line for the waterway.

The canal curved gently to the right to maintain its level, with the channel very wide at the bend. Close by the bank lay an old barge with an RB dragline excavator mounted on its after deck; it was flooded and lying on the canal bed and it did not look as if it would ever move from the spot. Joe looked at the maker's name on the dragline and commented that there was a certain irony in that it was called a Ruston Bucyrus. He was right; almost any time you see a Ruston machine nowadays it is exactly that – rustin'.

The railway had joined us for a brief while along here, before rattling away to the south again, taking the shortest possible route across the bog on its way to Mullingar. A small lake glinted through the trees in the distance to the north, and to the south the bog was peppered with a lot of scrub and birch trees.

The last mile to D'Arcy's bridge is spectacular. The parkland on the north of the canal is part of the Hyde Park demesne, with beautiful mature trees that were at their leafy best at this time of year. The gravel pathway gave way to a narrow tarmac road, and another good road appeared on the far bank, serving a small number of houses and farms. On our side we passed a few small cottages, with flower filled gardens in an idyllic setting, and the gentle curve of the canal reflected the line of tall trees on the far bank. We were both agreed that occasional stretches like this made the walk more than worthwhile.

At D'Arcy's bridge we crossed the canal again, stopping at a well-mown grass patch by the bridge to take on some more water; the sun was now high in the sky and we needed to keep drinking lots of liquids. Joe drank deeply from his water bottle, and I guessed that I would soon be donating one of my spare bottles to him; the drop left in his bottle would not get him as far as Mullingar.

Just beyond the bridge was a wide section of canal, probably designed as a turning place for barges. Two rusting barges, sitting on the canal bed with their metal plates sprung and looking to be well beyond repair, now occupied the space. These are the remains of the fleet owned by the Leech family, the last traders to operate cargo boats on the canal before it closed for business.

A gravely road brought us to the harbour at Thomastown, the

bridge and lock here marking the end of the long level that we had entered at Ferran's Lock the previous day. Along here some months previously I had met a woman walking along the bank on a Sunday afternoon, and we had struck up a conversation about the canal. She had told me that her name was Pamela Cooney, and that she lived nearby. She recalled how a man called Ian Bath had persuaded some local people to get involved in saving the canal from extinction some twenty years before. The local priest in Killucan had read out a notice after mass one Sunday, asking for volunteers, and she had put her name forward. A local group was formed, and for several years they worked hard to restore this section of canal, including the staircase of locks from here to the summit level at Mullingar. These eight locks, known collectively as the Killucan Flight, were crucial to the fate of the canal, leading as they did up to the summit level and the all-important feeder from Lough Owel. This restoration project was therefore one of the more crucial steps towards the eventual restoration of the entire waterway. Those of us who enjoy the waterway today owe a great debt of gratitude to people like Ian Bath and Pamela Cooney.

Joe's luck was in again, the harbour wall at Thomastown has a drinking water tap and he filled up his water bottle, as well as drinking several of cupped handfuls of water from the tap. I took the chance to top up my empties also; I was a bit concerned that Joe seemed to be suffering a bit in the heat, and a spare water supply would not go amiss. I knew also that there was a pub at Nead's Bridge where we would cross the N4 again at the summit level, so I was not too concerned about running out of drinking water altogether.

Thomastown Harbour is a nice spot to stop and take a rest. The harbour is a popular location for overnight mooring of canal cruisers, with a well-regarded pub on the far bank, and a slipway for access by boat owners. An important feeder from the Riverstown River enters the harbour close to where we were standing; this is controlled by an elaborate sluice arrangement on the river itself about a quarter of a mile away to the north. The harbour is also the headquarters of a canal cruiser hire company, whose boats we had seen at Castleknock on the first evening of our walk. The railway had come back to join us again, crossing the minor road at a level crossing just south of the bridge.

We picked up our packs and moved on, crossing the canal at the bridge to take the roadway on the southern bank. Both banks are passable for the next mile or so to Riverstown Bridge, but we had decided at the beginning of our walk to stick to the official route where possible.

We passed the 18th lock just beyond Thomastown Bridge. The road stepped up quickly along with the canal for the next mile, until we crossed over Riverstown Bridge, close to the old disused railway station that used to serve Killucan. Here we resumed our walk on the northern side, passing several locks in quick succession, bringing us quickly to the 25th lock just below Footy's Bridge. Beyond the bridge the grassy path again gave way to a narrow tarmac road; we were now on the highest level of the canal, more than 320 feet above the waters of the Liffey. From here the summit level runs all the way to the first descending lock, some 15 miles away at Coolnahay Harbour.

The little roadway along here was busy with strollers out enjoying the summer sunshine, and several anglers had set up their rods in the shade of the big trees near Footy's Bridge. We trudged on, both of us now feeling the heat and losing a lot of perspiration. The road and canal curved gently to the left as we walked, eventually bringing us into a construction site where a new motorway bridge was being built across the canal. Luckily on this Sunday afternoon there were no restrictions on access to the site; the last thing we wanted at this stage was any kind of diversion that would add distance to our journey.

The new bridge across the canal and this side road was being built so as to allow plenty of room for boat traffic on the canal, a far cry from the era when the existing Nead's bridge just ahead was being widened in the mid 1970s. At that time the canal had been written off by officialdom, and the proposed bridge would not have been wide enough to allow the passage of pleasure craft. There was no good reason for this attitude; the bridge would have to be raised in any case to cross the railway line, so the extra cost of providing a wide opening for the canal would have been minimal.

The Minister of the time finally conceded that the lobbying by the Inland Waterways Association was valid, and he asked the local authority to widen the bridge. This was a major victory for the voluntary sector in their fight to have the canal restored, and thereafter all bridges over the canal were made navigable. Two years later, when the road widening works were put in place beside Furey's pub in Moyvalley, a navigable bridge was included as part of the project. It would take a further twenty-five years however before the culverted road crossings at Mullingar and elsewhere would start to be removed and the navigation restored, and even as we walked this way in 2004 there were still several of these bars to navigation in place.

We stumbled up the rise to the N4, making a beeline for the open door of the pub by the roadside. We climbed on to two stools and ordered large cold drinks; we were now eighteen miles from our starting point and feeling the heat. We still had seven and a half miles to go, and I was feeling a bit guilty for not levelling with Joe – he thought that at this stage that we were much closer to Mullingar.

We sat and watched the football on the television for a while, then finished our drinks and moved outside, crossing the road to pick up the route on the far side and switching again to the south bank of the canal. When this bridge over the canal was eventually widened, it was made just big enough to allow a boat to pass, but no provision was made for walkers, or indeed for anyone who might want to tow a horse-drawn barge along the way in the future. The end result of this petulant approach by the County Council meant that walkers along the Royal Canal Way had to cross a very busy main road, taking their chances with speeding traffic. Now at least, the new motorway link road built to the rear of the pub has superseded the existing N4, leaving this crossing point much safer for pedestrian traffic.

The next section of canal is embanked, running through boggy terrain, and crossing a small river not far from the roadway. The canal bank carries a gravel roadway that serves some of the houses ahead on the left of the canal. As we crossed the little river we could see another large diesel powered pump at work, lifting water from the river to top up the level in the canal.

The angular shape of a drawbridge came gradually into view ahead of us; this structure was built to allow the houses on the left to have direct access to the N4 without having to travel down the road along which we had just walked. According to local lore, this drawbridge was erected as a compromise to get local farmers to remove a dam they had built to carry a farm road across the derelict canal, and the bridge was provided by the local authority in order to get the canal restored with the minimum of trouble. In hindsight, the authorities should probably have insisted that the trespassing farmers remove their blockage of the canal without the provision of any alternative; the road we had just walked gives adequate access to this area, as does its continuing stretch to the Downs Bridge further on. If a compromise had to be agreed, it should have been for the provision of a footbridge; currently boaters have to raise this drawbridge in order to pass this way, and then lower it behind them when they have gone through.

As happens far too often in Ireland, the canal bank along here gave repose to a number of rusting and dilapidated farm machines, and a partly dismantled tractor blocked the route, still lying in the same place where it had been when I walked here three months earlier. There are litter laws that apply to such situations, but quite often they are not adequately enforced. Hopefully the new farming regulations relating to environmental issues will help clean up eyesores like this.

Passing the scrap machinery, we carried on down the farm road, the canal moving away again from the roar of traffic on the N4. The boggy landscape had once again given way to good farmland, and tall trees shaded our route and kept the sun from our backs. The attractive Downs Bridge lay ahead, complete with a fully restored pair of stop gates, and we passed under the bridge on the towpath and carried on. The canal bent right, then left again, and now the dual carriageway of the N4 ran alongside on the far bank. A relatively recent footbridge loomed ahead, serving the small house on our left, and we decided to use its steps as a convenient stopping point for some food and drink.

Joe had been limping slightly for the past half-mile or so, and he used the rest stop as a chance to remove the offending boot and check the damage. He flicked a tiny pebble towards the canal, where it plopped noisily into the water; he had inadvertently picked it up some time back, probably where we crossed through the construction site for the new bridge, and he feared that it might have started a blister on his right foot.

We lingered for fifteen or twenty minutes at this bridge, giving our feet a rest and watching the heavy traffic speed by on the nearby road. We still had five miles to go, although Joe was blissfully unaware of this at this stage and thought that half an hour more would get him to Mullingar and a welcome rest.

The canal meandered again after the footbridge, moving away from the busy road and back into more peaceful countryside. The next stretch was carried on an embankment through some boggy land, with an abundance of furze and acid loving plants, but gradually we moved back to good farmland. The railway, which had moved away from us a couple of miles back, began to come back to join us, carried on its own embankment a couple of hundred yards away to the south.

The embankment gradually gave way to flatter ground, and then entered a cutting that slowly deepened as the land rose gradually. The next couple of miles had to be cut through a limestone hill reminiscent of the deep sinking at Porterstown, but the rock here was not as hard and did not present such severe difficulties for the canal builders. We passed Baltrasna Bridge, the last such crossing before Mullingar, and carried on through the now very high-sided cutting towards the town.

Beyond the bridge the canal swung right and left, and then settled into a slow curve to the right, creating a sense of expectation that we would suddenly round a corner and see Mullingar right in front of us. The setting sun was shining in our eyes, making it difficult for us to see ahead, and Joe was beginning to wonder aloud as to where Mullingar had disappeared. I kept encouraging him by telling him that it surely must not be far away now.

At last we emerged from the cutting and saw the town ahead, still some way off at the end of a straight stretch, so that a further fifteen minutes elapsed before we reached Saunder's Bridge and the town proper. The footpath here was busy, with a lot of young people out enjoying the summer evening. A small harbour just before Moran's Bridge had another hired canal boat moored for the night, with the occupants cooking up an appetizing dinner, at least as far as we could judge from the delicious smells emanating from the galley.

Moran's Bridge gave us both a pleasant surprise. The bridge was closed to navigation in the 1960s when the original bridge was demolished, and replaced with a culverted road crossing. We had not realized that the restoration of the navigation at this point was so far advanced, and we were pleased to see that the bridge deck had been raised and that canal boats could pass through here once more.

Our hotel was a tantalizing couple of hundred yards away up the street to our left, but we carried on past Moran's Bridge and followed the loop of the canal around the north of the town, where it runs on a high embankment. We crossed over a small stream and a pedestrian walkway, before coming to the point where the Lough Owel feeder enters the canal on a small embankment from the northwest, on the far bank from where we walked. This feeder, in reality a perfect miniature canal, carries the main supply of water for the canal over a distance of more than two miles from the lake. It enters the canal under a very attractively proportioned small stone bridge, designed to carry towing horses across the feeder.

Just past the feeder we came to the old harbour, its buildings somewhat derelict now, and we could see the old disused dry dock across the canal from us, but we did not linger here and hurried along. We crossed under Scanlan's Bridge, passing the site of many of the now demolished harbour warehouses, walking on under the remains of an old metal footbridge and under the railway line where it leaves Mullingar on its way towards Sligo. Muscles aching, we were glad to see Green Bridge ahead of us, and we turned left at the bridge and walked down the street towards the town centre and the Greville Arms Hotel. We had walked just over twenty-five miles since leaving Enfield, and I could feel the beginnings of a blister on my left foot. Joe was visibly flagging too, and we checked into the hotel and agreed to meet for dinner an hour later.

When I had booked this hotel a month earlier I hadn't banked on the County football team winning the Leinster championship on the same day as our stay. Neither had I factored in that the Hotel sponsors the team, and that the entire band of supporters seemed to have taken over the hotel bars and were settling in for an unforgettable celebration. All I could hope for at this stage was that my weariness would help me sleep through most of the racket.

A hot bath later and I didn't feel too bad, but my blisters had burst and the skin was completely abraded from the top of two of my toes on the left foot. I dressed them as best I could, but I was a bit concerned as to whether they would last for the next few days without letting me down altogether. I had fitted my boots with shock absorbing insoles to deal with a painful bone on the sole of one foot, but these insoles had obviously raised my feet to the point where the tops of the boots were causing abrasion damage.

When I met Joe later he had similar problems; the stone he had picked up had caused a painful blister on the sole of one foot, but he hoped to dress it sufficiently to carry him for two more days. He had made a decision however; he was only going to walk the length of the canal and not on to the coast as he had hoped. He was finding that the heat and the remnants of a bad flu were slowing him down, and he knew his limitations. I was disappointed but tried not to show it; I knew that there is strength in numbers and that I would need moral support if I was to get at least as far as my original target, the house at Clooncunny where the four Flannerys were born and raised, and from where they had set out to walk to Dublin.

I was beginning to develop a healthy respect for my four great grand uncles. They had made the journey on foot without the benefit of high tech boots or lightweight rucksacks and clothing. Not for them the luxury of spending the night in a comfortable hotel; they had to make do with whatever shelter they could find along the way, bedding down for the night in a hay barn or under a dry hedge. Food had to be either carried, in the form of dry oatcakes and salted bacon, or otherwise found in the fields as they passed along the way. I could picture them at the end of the day with their cooking pot over a camp fire, boiling up a piece of bacon with some potatoes from a field near the canal.

No such hardship for us; we retired to the dining room to eat. We were expecting it to be full, given the masses of supporters awaiting the return of the victorious team, but we need not have worried; they were all in the bar! We ordered our food from a slightly bewildered waitress who came back several times to check that she had got our order right. Eventually the food arrived and we demolished it hungrily. The service had been mediocre, although the food was reasonable, and I asked Joe whether he intended to give a tip to our waitress. "Yes", he said, "I'll tell her never to run with her shoelaces open". Still, I was glad to see that he was only joking and that he added a few euros to the total when he paid the bill.

I retired to bed for an early night, and Joe decided to check out the scene in the bar and have a pint with the now very noisy football supporters, whose sheer weight of numbers meant that the lobby and staircases had now become de facto extensions to the bars, so that I had to force my way through crowds of pint-bearing fans to get upstairs to my room.

6

Mullingar to Abbeyshrule

Beside yon straggling fence that skirts the way
With blossomed furze unprofitably gay
There, in his noisy mansion, skilled to rule
The village master taught his little school

The Deserted Village –
Oliver Goldsmith 1728–1774

It was a measure of the extent of my tiredness that the noise from the bar did not prevent me from sleeping. Neither did the arrival of the victorious team and the rest of the supporters at some later hour cause me any concerns; I heard nothing at all and had to rely on Joe's account the following morning over breakfast. His "one pint" had turned to two or three, and he had enjoyed a good night in the company of the happy football fans. The hotel dining room was not very busy, and we ate as much as we could manage; a journey of about 18 miles lay ahead of us before we would get to Abbeyshrule.

We discussed our progress so far as we ate our way through the large Irish breakfast. We had travelled just slightly less than 54 miles from Dublin, with about 36 miles to go to the end of the canal, and a further mile to the bridge over the Shannon at Tarmonbarry. We had passed the half way mark on the canal the previous afternoon close to the 25th lock and the start of the summit level, so for Joe at least, we were on the home stretch. I had not yet made a decision as to how far I would go by myself when Joe would leave at Tarmonbarry, but I still wanted to emulate the walk made by the Flannerys all those years ago, so I was still a good few miles short of my half way stage.

We collected our bags and checked out, crossing the road and heading up the street towards our point of departure from the canal the previous evening. We spotted a small delicatessen on the right hand side of the street, and we stopped off to buy some sandwiches and a few bottles of water (or just a bottle in Joe's case). We crossed back to the other side of the road and turned off along the footpath by the canal at Green Bridge.

The morning was nice for walking, but dark clouds were massing on the horizon and the blue sky was gradually obliterated; we were agreed that this would probably be a day for the rain gear. Conscious of the deteriorating weather, we set a fast pace away from the town to get as much walking done as possible before the rain moved in.

The canal bank along here is obviously well used by walkers, and a good footpath made the going easy. Several blocks of new apartments were in the course of completion along the bank; it is a measure of the way in which old commercial routes like canals have been accepted into the landscape as almost natural features, so that homes with a view of the waterway now command a premium. It is unlikely that such an accolade will be awarded to our motorways 200 years from now.

We left the town on a low embankment, with industrial buildings to the south and suburban housing to the north. The Sligo rail line had departed from us for good; it heads away to the north west from Mullingar, but a disused branch railway line still ran beside us here, just out of sight most of the time behind thick hedges. We walked under a new road bridge on the outskirts of the town. The line of the canal here is not the original; it was diverted slightly to allow for the construction of the road bridge, and we could still see the depression in the ground marking the original route. No doubt in another generation this will have been forgotten, and people will see the slight twist in the canal as just an attractive feature.

The branch line on our left, now disused, was the original Galway line that ran through Athlone. The sidings along the track were piled high with lifted sections of track, with sleepers attached, but the line itself appeared to be out of use. This reminded me of an interesting detail about Mullingar's railway history; railway lines in the early days of rail were laid in a simple way by bedding down the sleepers and laying the rails one at a time on the sleepers. Nobody had successfully managed to design a machine that would lay the complete sections of track in one piece, where the sections could be made up in the yard, transported to site and laid mechanically.

All that changed in the years immediately following the First World War; a railway engineer in Mullingar, Arthur White-Bretland, invented the Bretland track-laying system while stationed in the town. The basis of this system is still in use today. In 1924 when it came into use it revolutionised track laying, allowing half a mile of track to be laid in a single eight-hour shift.

Another little piece of railway history was made here; the signal box at Mullingar railway station, now replaced by a modern computerised system, was the setting for a scene in a film made about the great train robbery, starring Sean Connery.

There is a good footpath on both sides of the canal from here to Kilpatrick Bridge. The problems we had seen earlier with a lack of division between public and private land were not evident here; it was very obvious that the canal on both sides of the town was a treasured amenity that is respected and cared for by the local population. This stretch was well sheltered also, with high hedges on our side of the canal and more open farmland to the north. We passed a riding school, across from us on the far bank, with an instructor shouting commands at a group of youngsters on horseback.

We walked under Kilpatrick Bridge on the towpath and carried on along the same side towards Belmont Bridge, reaching it no more than ten minutes later, and we crossed back to the north side again to pick up the trail. We were already nearly three miles out of town and keeping up a good fast pace. Joe seemed to have recovered his stamina and was back in his usual place in front, while I kept my own pace to the rear, occasionally putting on a bit of a spurt to catch up.

There are two bridges at Ballinea; the original arched stone bridge and a newer concrete slab across the canal, but fortunately the latter was built so as to provide adequate access for boats. The old bridge is interesting in that it is a "skew" bridge, built to cross the canal at an angle. This is not simply a question of turning the bridge around to cross the canal at an angle; the bridge buttresses are offset from each other but are parallel to the bank, and the stonework is cut obliquely to transfer the load on to the buttresses. The system was developed by the Romans, and always fascinates me whenever I come across it.

There is a small harbour here before the bridge which would make a good mooring spot for the night, or provide a good turning place for a long narrow-boat, and a slipway allowing boaters to launch their craft. We had passed another slipway at Mullingar harbour the evening before; there are good facilities along here for boat owners.

The official way switched again here to the south bank, and we set off along what is a very grassy track, although it had been mown in the recent past and the going was not too bad. The rain was beginning to threaten, and we felt the occasional drops, but we kept moving quickly, deferring the decision to don the waterproofs for as long as possible. This stretch was blocked in a few places by what were obviously unofficial gates placed by local farmers; they were badly hung and did not show the solid workmanship of the Waterways Ireland crews. In one case we found one of these unofficial gates flattened along with its gateposts, obviously by an angry hiker. While we sympathised with the notion that this public way should be open to all, we were agreed that this was not the way to achieve such an end; allowing cattle to wander doesn't solve anything and only inflames the situation.

We crossed under the road at the recently built Shandonagh

Bridge, carrying the R392 road across the canal. The old bridge stood a few yards further along, and although the new bridge was of modern design it complimented the old bridge rather than clashed with it. We carried on along the same side on what was now a now fairly muddy track, obviously in use as a farm roadway. The dark clouds were threatening now, and about a mile further on the heavens opened and we ran for cover under a large sycamore tree. We sat out the shower here for about fifteen minutes, taking a drink of water and eating some chocolate, but it seemed that the rain might last for a while so we reluctantly decided to don the rain gear and carry on. Joe was organized quickly and disappeared down the path, while I dug to the bottom of the rucksack to find my waterproofs, eventually dragging on the hateful garments over my clothes. In spite of manufacturers' claims about "breathable fabrics", I always find that such garments trap perspiration and do nothing for my comfort, but anything was better than the rain that was at this stage drumming down incessantly.

As I repacked my bag I realized that this point was almost exactly half way to Clooncunny, and the thought occurred to me that if the Flannerys had set out from there at the same time as I had left Dublin, we would meet somewhere along here. I felt a kind of chill, as though I had seen a ghost, then I reprimanded myself for being irrational; they had passed here a hundred and forty years earlier. Still, I could not shake the feeling that I had just been in the presence of my four relatives; I felt closer to them right here than I had ever felt before. I wondered whether they had enjoyed dry weather for their journey, or if they had got a soaking in this open countryside, courtesy of our Irish summer weather.

I headed off into the rain, speeding up to gain on Joe as he disappeared into the murk. I caught up with him at the pretty Colnahay harbour, a place that would be idyllic on a good day, but today was miserable and uninviting. This place also marked the end of the summit level; the 26th lock just before the bridge would be the first one to start the process of stepping the canal down to the Shannon at Cloondara. The harbour had plenty of mooring and a good number of private craft were tied up, and several families of ducks were protesting loudly at being disturbed as we walked by. Joe was somewhat optimistically trying to take pictures with his digital camera, but I kept my head bowed to allow the rain to pour away from the hood of my jacket.

We did not dally long, striding on past the next two locks to get to the high and narrow Walsh's Bridge. The two lock houses we passed were falling down; the first was almost completely in ruins, and the second was not far behind. This one had had a wooden porch added to the front at some time, obviously the occupier's attempt to stop the heat disappearing every time he came out to open the lock gates. Now the porch was falling forward, away from the house, and the house itself seemed likely to follow soon after.

This is a pleasant enough stretch of the canal, but nowhere looks its best in heavy rainfall and we just kept our heads down and kept walking. Beyond Walsh's Bridge the waterway took a sharp left hand turn, and a level twisting section brought us a further mile to Kildallan Bridge. The canal then began to drop sharply and we passed four further locks over the next half-mile or so to Kill Bridge. The lock houses along here had been restored and extended and were in use; it was strange that in some cases these homes were valued and maintained, while a few hundred yards away they were allowed to fall down.

The canal swung suddenly to the left before Kill Bridge, and then bent around to the right again to pick up more or less the original line after the 33rd lock. A further straight stretch, less than a mile long, brought us to the 34th lock and the wide span of Balroe Bridge. We had noticed that the canal for the past few miles appeared to be meandering, as if trying to hug the contours of the land to avoid too much embanking or cutting,

The rain was easing off a little as we hit the long straight stretch of gravel road west of the bridge, where the canal was carried on a slight embankment through flat open countryside. The embankment disappeared as we dropped again at the next lock, the 35th just at the entrance to Ballynacargy harbour. We diverted through a landscaped section of ground beside the harbour and walked into the village to stock up on drinks and refreshments.

Ballynacargy is now a place that can only be described as sleepy, but at one time it was an important centre for trade on the canal. Following the completion of the works from Thomastown to the summit level and Mullingar, necessary to secure the good water supply from Lough Owel, the next phase drove the canal through Ballynacargy to the Inny River, and the little town grew up around what was then a major business centre on the waterway. The large harbour here provided mooring facilities for trade and passenger boats plying the route to Dublin.

Nowadays you would be forgiven for wondering about the reason for the existence of a village in this isolated place. The streets were practically deserted, with just a few young children playing an aimless game of football, and a solitary farmer drove a tractor slowly up the street, swivelling his head in order to maintain a fixed gaze on the two bedraggled walkers as we divested ourselves of our rainwear at a convenient bench outside "the Canal End" bar.

We broke out the sandwiches and had lunch; the sun was breaking through the clouds and drying away the worst effects of the rain and the food and drink cheered us up. Joe had the camera out again; the pub's name sign was too interesting to pass without committing it to the camera's memory. We stocked up again on snacks and drinks at the small supermarket, and headed back down the small side street to rejoin the canal. We had set a fast pace all morning; the miserable weather had deterred us from poking around at interesting places we passed, and we had travelled nearly twelve miles since we left our hotel three hours earlier. Something less than six miles of walking lay ahead before Abbeyshrule and an early night; this was going to be a relatively easy day.

We paused at the bridge to take stock of the surroundings. At the western end of the harbour a small stream trickled away under the approach road to the canal bridge; at first we thought it might be flowing the other way, providing a "top-up" to the waters of the canal, but the more we studied it the more its significance became obvious to us. In the canal's early years, when the harbour beside us formed the end of one of the stages in the canal's extension from Coolnahay to the Inny, an overflow was needed to carry away surplus water from the harbour. Each time a lock was used on the section from the summit level down to here it sent several tons of water flowing downstream; nowadays this simply flows onwards towards the Inny and Shannon via the completed canal, but at that time an overflow point was needed to prevent the harbour constantly flooding until the next section was completed as far as the Inny river. The presence of this small stream had helped determine where a stage of the canal could be temporarily terminated until the rest of that section was constructed.

We crossed the bridge and set off again along the slightly embanked footpath, more a wide roadway really, beside what was also now a wide waterway. The day had brightened up considerably and we were both in good humour, with only our blisters giving cause for concern. The land on either side of the canal was flat and fertile, although we knew that a further hour's walk would bring us through poor bogland, which had proved a difficult challenge for the builders of the canal.

We were both confident now that we would easily reach the canal end at Cloondara the next day, regardless of whether or not our blistered feet got any worse. Joe even called his wife Pauline and made arrangements to meet there on the following evening. We had now put more than two thirds of the canal behind us, and in my case I had well passed the half way mark on my goal of reaching Clooncunny. I began to daydream as I followed behind Joe, who was now moving ahead again and was maintaining a lead of about 100 yards on me; I thought about how the Flannerys would now be coming in to the outskirts of Mullingar if they had left home at the same time as I did. I hoped that their feet had not given them too much trouble with blisters; it was bad enough to be walking across the country in order to emigrate to a new life without the misery of painful feet. Over the past few days I had irrationally begun to think of their journey as contemporaneous with mine, and not as something that happened a hundred and forty years earlier.

The countryside here was quiet and still, with no sign of anybody working in the fields and no traffic noise from the road away to the north of us. We both began to slow down a little, not under any pressure to get anywhere fast, and I drew alongside Joe and we strolled and chatted for a couple of miles. We passed the 36th lock with its two-storey lock house; the original house had obviously been extended over the years. A small "bridge to nowhere" stood just beyond it – an accommodation bridge that had been built to serve a landowner whose land was divided by the canal. This bridge looked stark in the landscape; its walls were truncated at the bank and not turned to form the access roadway as with normal road bridges, and it looked somewhat unfinished by comparison.

Kiddy's Bridge, carrying a small side road steeply across the canal followed soon after, followed by another accommodation bridge with a lock on either side of it. The canal was dropping here almost as quickly as it had risen on the Killucan Flight beyond Mullingar. This bridge deck was grassy and little used by the look of it, and a yellow steel barrier to prevent vehicle access blocked the roadway along the bank. The lock keeper's cottage had almost completely fallen down and the remainder of the building was overgrown with briars.

I paused to look at the disused lock keeper's cottage at the 38th lock. One of my most treasured books is Ruth Delany's "Ireland's Royal Canal", a most interesting history of the canal over two centuries. A small photograph in the book pictures one Patrick Byrne, who was the lock keeper here in the 1950s. The photograph was taken on a fine summer day, and the subject is squinting slightly as he looks directly into the sunlight for the camera. A collie dog has flopped to the ground behind him, and a few hens peck at the dust in front of the open cottage door. A bicycle is propped against the cottage wall, the whole scene a study in tranquillity. Patrick Byrne is dressed in his best clothes for the picture, and it conjures up memories of another, simpler age. The cottage now stands empty and forlorn; a broken gable window allowing the weather to deteriorate the building still more, and the memory of the happy picture brought a cloud to my day.

For some reason the name stone had been removed from Kelly's Bridge, forced out from its surrounding stone frame, and on the far side of the bridge the stone had also been removed. We were puzzled as to why this would have been done; surely no one would steal the name from a bridge?

Ledwith's Bridge was another accommodation bridge, then shortly afterwards we were out in the beautiful open panorama of Ballymaglavy Bog. The canal ran almost straight through the bog; difficulties with the waterway's construction along here related to the nature of the soil, but the flat terrain meant that one line was as good as another when the canal's course was being set out. We passed over the Blackwater, more a small stream than a river at this time of year, feeding the River Inny just off to the north; its culverted route under the canal was marked by a wooden railing along the pathway.

Ahead of us in the distance we could see a high stone bridge, dominating the horizon in this flat landscape. This is called the Bog Bridge, and seems to have been built without purpose, since it now serves no roadway and has fallen into disuse. As we got closer we could see that the bridge roadway was completely overgrown with high grass and weeds; it was apparent that nobody had crossed over it in a long time. It is a beautiful structure, with carefully executed stonework evident throughout its construction; the bridge walls are finished off at each end with squared cut stone piers that would not be out of place in the grounds of a stately home. It is amazing that a purely utilitarian structure such as this, built two hundred years ago in the middle of a bog, would have been given such embellishment; the people who put this waterway in place were building for posterity, and took real pride in their work.

This bridge, we were to find out later from a local taxi driver, was very important when the bog around here was in commercial production over the previous couple of centuries. At one time, he told us, there were twelve houses along a bog road that crossed over this bridge and served the bog here, all of the families making a good living from cutting and saving turf. Now not a trace of these houses remains, and the bridge looks as though it was dropped here from outer space, such is its impact in the wild landscape of the bog.

We were in no hurry to get to Abbeyshrule, now only half an hour away, so we dug out the rest of our snacks and drinks and sat down for a rest on the dry spongy bank on the leeward side of the bridge, enjoying our impromptu picnic in the now warm afternoon sunshine. We lay back on the comfortable and dry ground, watching the small clouds scud across the blue sky, and Joe was soon snoring as he caught up on his sleep deficit of the previous night. I decided to let him sleep for half an hour; I was in no hurry to leave this beautiful and restful spot.

I became aware of the men walking on the other bank before I saw them, and they gradually came into view from my left, walking purposefully towards us from the direction of Abbeyshrule. There were four tall men in long coats, walking quickly in single file, each of them carrying a bundle on his shoulder. The man in front was very tall, well over six feet, and powerfully built, with wavy fair hair and a large old-fashioned moustache decorating a friendly face. He stopped just opposite us, and the other three caught up with him one by one and dropped their bundles, sitting down gratefully on the bank for a short rest. The big man stayed standing and his bundle seemed not to weigh heavily on him, it remained on his shoulder as he spoke.

"I'm Brian Flannery", he said, "and these are the brothers" "We're heading for Dublin."

"I know", I said. "I thought you'd be further on by now".

He laughed. "These lads are a bit slow", he said. "Not used to hardship. You're going well yourself anyway, but why wouldn't you, and you a Flannery? You'll have no bother getting to Clooncunny, but I have my doubts about the landlord's boy". He motioned to the sleeping form of Joe. "Still, he said, "they're certainly not used to hardship, but they're not the worst, the McDermotts."

"No", I said, "They're not the worst".

He motioned to the three brothers. "Come on boys, enough of this lying around, we need to be off". They got reluctantly to their feet and hoisted their bundles, and the little convoy headed off to the east. Brian looked over his shoulder as he departed. "Tell them in Clooncunny that we are all well here", he said, and then he was gone.

I awoke suddenly; Joe was still snoring away on the bank beside me. The dream had been so vivid that I looked across the canal in the direction of Ballynacargy, still half expecting to see the four Flannerys marching off to Dublin and their new life. I needed to get a grip. I gave Joe a nudge and he sat up suddenly; "I wasn't asleep," he said, "just closing my eyes for a minute to rest".

I looked at my watch; we must have slept for nearly an hour in the warm sunshine. We got stiffly to our feet and moved on, taking short stiff-legged steps for a while until the muscles began to free up and we got back to our usual pace. Despite the snacks and the lunch we were both feeling the first pangs of hunger; there is something about the air out on the bog that seems to whet the appetite, and we began to discuss the possibilities for our evening meal in Abbeyshrule.

On an earlier visit to the village I had been given the telephone number of a woman who ran a bed and breakfast business, but repeated phone calls to her this afternoon had not elicited any reply; still, we were not too worried, there were bound to be others, and the people in the pub in Abbeyshrule would put us right.

The bog here was beautiful, marred only by a number of abandoned cars beside the pathway. In rural Ireland in the past, there was a tradition of burying the year's rubbish under the spreading ground when the turf bank was being cleaned in preparation for the turf cutting each spring. In those less material times, a year's waste from an average household consisted of a sack or two containing a few broken bottles and maybe a few tin cans, a far cry from today's weekly bin collections of the detritus of modern living. Unfortunately in some places the bog is still seen as a place to dump unwanted items, and not always appreciated as the wonderful landscape that it actually is. Although an increasing awareness of the value of the environment is emerging in rural Ireland, the occasional person still despoils the landscape in this manner.

We were still on the south bank of the canal, and the pathway gave way to a narrow tarmac road, which left us again very soon afterwards, crossing the canal over Quinn's Bridge. The River Inny could be glimpsed in the near distance across the canal, and we could also see the small airfield of the Abbeyshrule flying club; as we walked a small plane landed on the runway. This runway was described to me some years previously as "a skid mark in a field" by a pilot friend from the UK; more used to the large airfields on his home patch, he had flown in to Abbeyshrule one weekend and was nervous about landing there.

We approached the aqueduct over the River Inny, a very impressive structure with five stone arches, carrying not only the canal but also a small roadway on either side of the waterway. It is said that the Whitworth Aqueduct is best viewed from the riverbank below, but we resolved to do this at another time, a good dinner now being uppermost in our thoughts. We leaned over the low wall beside the roadway to try and see as much as possible of the structure from above. Another huge diesel-powered pump was roaring away here, pumping water up from the river to bring up the level in that section of canal.

Across the aqueduct the canal swung hard left, with just a straight stretch remaining as far as Abbeyshrule, carried on a high embankment. Off to our right across the canal we could see a picture-perfect thatched cottage, complete with small red painted wooden windows and a single white chimney. We were walking on the roadway now and not higher up on the bank proper, but we decided to stay at the lower level and walked into the village along the road. The "Old Rustic Inn" is Abbeyshrule's well-known watering hole, situated right beside the canal embankment, and we turned gratefully in the doorway and dropped our bags by the counter.

The friendly young woman behind the bar produced a menu, and we made a selection and ordered drinks. While we waited on the food we enquired as to the local landlady and the possibilities for a bed for the night, only to be told that she was on holiday in America and would be away for another week. Our new friend began to call other establishments in the immediate area, but these were all full; it seemed that we would have to revise our plans somewhat.

7

Abbeyshrule to Termonbarry

Wild river! How my heart is beating now
All – all my dreams by thee are dead and gone
Thy country wears the death-cloud on its brow
Thy loneliness the emblem of her son

The Inny – a contrast.
John Keegan Casey 1846–1870

We examined our options over the very tasty dinner in Abbeyshrule's "Old Rustic Inn." We could walk another six miles to Chaigneau Bridge near Ballymahon; surely such a town would have a few choices with regards to accommodation. Alternatively we could get a taxi to either Ballymahon or to one of the other larger towns, stay in whatever accommodation we could find, and get a taxi back to Abbeyshrule in the morning. We were pretty much agreed on one thing, the option of walking further was not for us, we had mentally switched off for the day when we dropped our bags in the pub and only a real emergency would have coaxed us back on the trail again. The young woman passed us a copy of the local telephone directory and we began calling hotels and guesthouses. She also told us that she knew a reliable taxi man who could take us to wherever we wanted, and collect us in the morning.

It is one of life's great mysteries that spokespersons for the hotel and tourism sector are almost invariably downbeat, always complaining that they are going practically out of business because each year is worse than the last; yet whenever you want to find a room anywhere, they are all full. Such was the case in Ireland's midlands on this summer evening, but we finally got lucky with a grand-sounding hotel that was not too far distant.

"Forty five euro each for bed and breakfast" the receptionist on the other end of the phone told me; we agreed and made the two reservations. We finished our meal with a generous and tasty apple crumble, and almost on cue our taxi arrived.

The recommendation was good; Michael was a friendly fellow with a wealth of local information about the canal and the bogs, and he charged us a very reasonable 17 euro for the trip to the hotel. He would have no problem collecting us in the morning, he said, but it would have to be at 8.30 as he had an existing commitment at 9.00 in Ballymahon. It was a little earlier than we had planned, but not a problem, so we agreed to see him outside the hotel door at 8.30 sharp.

When we checked in we enquired about the time for breakfast; it was from 8.30 the receptionist told us, but we could have the "continental breakfast" at any time after 7.00. We were happy enough with that; a good continental breakfast would sustain us for a day's walk, and we could still meet our taxi on time.

I retired to my room to have a hot bath and watch some TV, while Joe headed for a quick nightcap in the bar. The room was fairly spartan, only boasting a very basic shower, but I managed to bathe my damaged feet as best I could and I slept soundly.

I awoke at 7.30 and headed down to breakfast, giving a bang on Joe's door as I passed. The only staff member to be seen downstairs was a young barman, cleaning up the floor of the bar with a small brush and a dustpan. I asked him directions to the dining room and he gestured to his left with the full dustpan, spilling some of the contents in the process. As I walked in the direction he had shown he called after me, "there's no breakfast, she doesn't come in for a good while yet".

I remonstrated with him; the receptionist had advised me that the continental option was available much earlier. Slowly he seemed to remember something about such things, "there's some shtuff beyont there all right," he said, pointing again with the dustpan. I walked to the end of the room, but could only see a few bowls containing cereal, covered with cling-film. I turned to ask the young man as to where the rest of the "shtuff" could be found, but he was right behind me, still carrying his brush and dustpan.

"Milk?" I said, "tea and coffee? Fruit juice? Bread?"

He smiled nervously, "there'd be none of that shtuff yet" he said, "She doesn't come in for a good while yet".

"No milk even?" I said.

"Hould on", he said, leaving down his cleaning tools on one of the tables. He wiped his hands on the front of his trousers and rummaged under the food counter until he found a large glass milk jug, with a few millimetres of milk left in it from the day before, clinging to the sides of the glass as he tilted it for a better look. He studied this for a while, seeming to come to the realisation that this was not enough for two breakfasts, then he thought again and went to the large milk dispenser and put the jug under it. He pulled on the tap and added about half a pint of milk to the stale milk already in the jug, smiling triumphantly as he presented me with the result.

I tried to make the best of things. "Now", I said, "All we need is bread and butter, fruit juice, and a pot of tea"

His face fell again; "she doesn't come in...."

"For a good while yet", I said, "I know that, is there a shop where I can buy the makings of a breakfast?"

He pointed me up the street to a small shop that was indeed open; they had no bread but I bought two cartons of orange juice and walked back to the hotel. At this stage Joe was wandering around looking for his breakfast, and getting the same answers as I had got. He brightened up at the sight of the cold cartons of juice, and we ate a couple of bowls of cereal each and drank from the cartons.

It was after eight at this stage, and I volunteered to go up the street to see whether the supermarket was open, and to get some sandwiches for the journey. It was just opening its doors, and I made a beeline for the delicatessen counter at the rear. A lively young woman was just setting up behind the counter; she had a name badge, obviously supplied by the company, which told me that her name was Linda. In addition, she wore a gold necklace with "Linda" hanging from it in gold letters. "Good morning Linda", I said, "can I have four ham sandwiches on brown bread, and can you wrap them in two packages?"

"Oh howya", she said, looking at me with a slightly puzzled expression, as if unsure as to how I knew her name, but not wanting to seem impolite at not recognizing me. She asked me to pass her a fresh brown loaf from the bread racks behind me, and she started to slice some nice looking fresh ham. She passed me the two packs of food, and leaned conspiratorially towards me. "I'm just charging you for two sandwiches with double fillings" she said. You obviously get better service when you know people around here!

I walked quickly back to the hotel and did a fast bit of packing. To her credit, the receptionist rounded the room charge down by a miserable enough five euros when I told her of the lack of breakfast, and I managed to intercept Joe before he checked out so that she applied the same discount to his bill. He had been using his head even at this early hour, and had gone back to the room where he had used the tea making facilities to get his essential morning cuppa.

True to his word, Michael pulled up exactly on time as promised and we headed for Abbeyshrule. We told him of our experiences and he was dismayed; as with ourselves, he thought that such poor service belonged in another age altogether, and he resolved never to recommend that hotel to any of his passengers in the future. In spite of having a deadline to meet, he stopped at a shop along the way to allow us to purchase the snacks and water that we had not had time to get in the supermarket.

Michael's friendly service and helpful manner cheered us up after our irritating experience in the hotel, and when he dropped us at the culvert by the canal in Abbeyshrule our good humour had returned and we were able to make light of the whole matter. It would take more than one badly managed hotel to spoil what was so far proving to be a great trip along the Royal Canal.

It was still cool enough to keep our sweaters on as we set off from the culverted road crossing at Abbeyshrule. The local authority at some time in the sixties had solved the problems of traffic trying to negotiate the narrow canal bridge in the village by building a road across the bed of the canal, effectively blocking the route to boat traffic, with just a few concrete pipes laid under the road along the line of the canal to water to flow past. Now however moves were afoot to raise all such crossings and to restore the canal to full navigation, and we had heard that this particular crossing would be the next to be removed and replaced with a high bridge. As we set off on our walk however this point marked the end of navigation from Dublin.

The original bridge was only a few minutes walk downstream; an attractive high arched stone structure that thankfully had survived the onslaught of the local authority. We paused for a minute on the top of the bridge to look around; the next time we looked back here we hoped, the culvert would be just a memory. Looking west, the canal broadened into a small harbour just beyond the bridge, and the area had been landscaped and decorated with a miniature thatched-cottage. Joe committed the scene to digital memory and we headed west.

The canal turned sharply right just beyond the bridge, and then started a long slow curve back to the left all the way to the next landmark, the 39th lock just before Draper's Bridge. The canal bank along the stretch to Draper's Bridge was lined with tall trees, and the area around the lock was stoned and tidy. The lock keeper's cottage here was partly ruined, and clearly it would soon be almost beyond restoration.

Just south of Draper's Bridge there is a fine stone bridge across the River Inny, and the ruins of a magnificent cut stone mill building lie just beyond the bridge on the south bank of the river. This area is called Tenelick, and was famous for it's milling for many years until the mill was burned down sometime around 1920, a deed said to have been done by the "black and tans", the English auxiliaries with their distinctive brown and black uniforms and their penchant for cruelty.

John Keegan Casey, one of Ireland's best loved poets and the author of many well known poems and ballads, spent much of his tragically short life in this part of the world, in the environs of the Royal Canal. For a brief period he was a clerk in the mill at Tenelick, working in an office on the right hand side of the building as you approach it from the canal, from where he could see the River Inny tumbling past outside his window.

We were still on the south bank of the canal, which twisted slightly after the lock, and which was by now raised on an embankment to maintain the level. A couple of hundred yards on we noticed what appeared to be a stone apartment building on the far bank. We stopped and looked at the building, unsure of whether it was a house with a large balcony upstairs or whether it was what the Americans call a "two-family home".

The River Inny came close to the path on our left a little further on; just one small field separated the canal from the river at this point, with the canal running at a higher level on the embankment, which by now was level with the roof of one house as we passed. The stretch of canal between this lock and the next one at Mullawornia, some seven miles away, is the longest level on the downhill side of the canal. In addition to the use of embankments it achieves this largely by following the contours of the land instead of trying to drive a straight line across the landscape, resulting in a more twisting course than we had seen so far.

We carried on along the same side, although there was no way-marker of any kind to define the route of the Royal Canal Way. The road was narrow, but nice for walking, and the surface gradually gave way to a grassy path. This place was pleasant, with frequent twists and bends, as well as a lot of bridges, breaking the journey into manageable pieces and keeping our interest up at this early stage of the day. From Draper's Bridge to Allard's Bridge we followed a roadway that crossed over the bridge, leaving us unsure which way to proceed. I fished around in my rucksack and found the Waterways Ireland guide to the canal, a small wire bound book which we had found to be a mine of interesting information about the canal, and which had good maps with the walkable footpaths marked on them.

The guide told us that we could stay on the same side all the way, or cross here and stay with the road along the northern bank. We decided to stay on the same side, passing the bridge and following the tight left-hand bend just a few minutes further on. The waterway was by now beginning to twist and turn sharply each few hundred yards, sticking to the contours of the rolling hills that make up the landscape here. A short walk brought us to Guy's Bridge, then the canal swung hard right again and the quaintly named Molly Ward's Bridge came into view; just beyond this bridge the canal took a sudden hard left turn. There were still no way markers, so we continued along the same side, passing the bridge and a stone spillway covered by a new concrete arch and protected by wooden handrails. The roadway deteriorated to become a fairly overgrown grassy bank along the canal, which meandered in every direction for the next mile or so to Fowlard's Bridge. The twisting nature of the canal over the morning's walk, far from being an irritant, made for a very pleasant journey; long straight stretches can be soul destroying as you look ahead and only see the path stretching away into the distance, but the frequent bends meant that we never knew what to expect around the next corner.

We took a rest stop at Fowlard's Bridge, an ugly looking concrete slab that had been built to replace the earlier stone bridge, but at least the waterway's navigable status had been maintained. We noticed an angular bracket carrying a water main across the bridge. Joe pointed out the danger that this protruding bar created for an unwary boat owner passing this way; it would be very easy to give yourself a severe blow on the head with this obstacle if you were not alert to such dangers.

A small cottage on the bank here by the bridge was being extended and renovated to make a nice home for somebody; it was a pity that the original bridge had not survived to complete the picture here.

We debated again as to which side to take beyond the bridge; the absence of way markers was becoming a slight irritant, and the Waterways Ireland guidebook indicated both banks as being walkable. I had walked the right bank a few months before and found it passable, but with high wet grass in places, but the southern side didn't seem any better and we decided to go with the northern bank. We passed through a gate after a few minutes, and then the surface began to deteriorate somewhat, with high weeds. It was dry enough however and we made good progress.

The morning was staying fine, if heavily overcast and it did not look as though we were in for much more than an occasional shower. We moved off along the gently curving bank that brought us to Toome Bridge, crossing over the bridge again to pick up the path on the southern side. I walked ahead of Joe, following the ramped roadway down from the bridge and turning right along the bank. I was surprised to see him ahead of me; he had spotted a stile set into the bridge wall that I had missed, costing me twenty yards of precious distance!

Toome Bridge was a busy place in days gone by, in stark contrast to its present day sleepy state. Bianconi's "long cars"— horse drawn cars that introduced scheduled passenger road services to the country — carried passengers by road from Athlone to connect with the passenger boats here for onward travel to Dublin.

We moved off again, setting a target of Island Bridge near Keenagh for our lunchtime stop. Joe was in good form, but was by now tending to fall behind me rather than lead. I was beginning to feel very fit, and apart from my damaged feet I felt that I could walk forever.

Fifteen minutes walk brought us to Chaigneau Bridge, and we were surprised to find the pathway under the bridge blocked off, the stile here had been wired shut. The canal was full of reeds here, and a raft made from oil drums was tied up along the bank just below the bridge. The old lock keeper's cottage on our left, now roofed with asbestos sheeting, seemed to be occupied. Several caravans were parked alongside the house, and a high wire mesh fence enclosed the house and caravans. Behind the fence a number of dogs snarled and growled at us as we passed up the ramped path to the bridge roadway. The gate provide by Waterways Ireland at the roadside was of the usual sturdy pattern, with a space beside it to allow walkers to squeeze through. A small wicket gate tied with wire had blocked this space, and the gate itself had been sheeted with wire mesh. We untied the small wicket gate to allow us to pass, tying it again behind us when we got through. Somebody around here did not want walkers to walk the Royal Canal Way. I was back here a few months later for a Saturday afternoon stroll and I found the little wicket gate nailed shut and secured by several padlocks.

Ballybrannigan Harbour is one of those places that invites a short stop and a bit of exploration. The canal widens beyond the bridge to form a large harbour, which was an important centre in the heyday of the canal. Joe had his camera out again, photographing the detail on the beamed upper floor of a canal side warehouse. Further along, the old waiting room for canal boat passengers has been renovated by a local employment scheme, and the bank and quays around the harbour have also been cleaned up and restored.

The road that peeled off to the left led to Ballymahon, and we carried on along the stony pathway on the southern bank. The route swung hard right beyond the harbour, and then ran straight ahead to a bend where we could hear machinery running. As we approached the curve in the canal we could see that a large earthen dam ahead blocked the canal, marking the end of the watered section. Beyond the dam, the canal was empty and forlorn looking, and the pump we had heard was pumping the dregs of water up from the almost dry bed beyond the dam.

Major repair work to the channel and banks was obviously under-way here. The pathway was deeply rutted from the tracks of excavators, and was sticky underfoot where the soil had been recently levelled out. We made our way carefully along for the next half mile to where a culvert led under the R392 road from Longford to Ballymahon, at the site of the former Longford Bridge.

Just before the roadway there was a temporary site office and associated huts belonging to Waterways Ireland; their crews were obviously tackling this next stretch to prepare it for re-watering. A couple of tracked excavators were parked on the bank, and a large tracked dumper sat on the other side of the canal. The channel as far as the road had been scraped clean by an excavator bucket, and had been lined with clay, and we could see another excavator a few hundred yards ahead at work on pulling scrub and waste from the canal bed.

This culvert will also have to be removed to allow boats to pass, but we had heard that this was due to happen within the next year or so. We crossed the road and walked along, stopping to chat to the crew who were working with the excavator further on, near Archie's Bridge. They were using a tracked excavator with an unusually long arm to clean and shape the canal bed. They were curious to know what we were doing, and were amazed that we had walked the nearly eighty miles from Dublin. They were even more astounded when we told them that we had done it in a total of about four days so far. They said that they often met walkers along the canal, but that these would seldom have walked the route in one go, usually picking it off in short stretches over time.

We complimented them on the work done so far, and they seemed pleased. They were genuinely interested in seeing the canal brought back into use, and were happy to be involved in its restoration. They wished us luck with the rest of our journey, and we left them still scratching their heads at the notion of two middle-aged men walking all the way from Dublin. "I would think hard about driving that distance", said one of them as we departed.

It felt strange walking beside the dry canal, and we felt a bit lonesome for the shining water that had been our companion since we left Dublin. "A canal without water" said Joe profoundly, "isn't the same at all". The other thing that was evident was the sheer depth of the canal; up to now we had seen the bottom in places as we walked, but it now appeared that refraction had made it appear much shallower than it actually was. The dry canal here was deep, so much so that it would be difficult to climb out of it along this steep sided section if you slipped in.

The repair crews had evidently not reached the section beyond Archie's Bridge, and the canal bed and the banks were overgrown with scrub and small trees. The path was passable with ease, but the canal itself was in a sorry state. Years of neglect had allowed the channel to become badly overgrown, but local effort had managed to keep the pathway open, and some specimen trees had been planted on the left hand side of the route. Despite the badly neglected appearance, we figured that this section could be brought back into use quickly if the culvert at Longford Bridge were to be lifted.

We had crossed the roadway half a mile back, and the repair crew had joked that we were putting extra effort on ourselves – the canal was swinging around in a wide loop and would cross the road again further on. They had suggested that we could cheat a little and walk the much shorter distance to Pake Bridge by road. Not a chance! We were determined to walk every inch of this beautiful canal, even the dry bits.

The canal was bending to the right all the time after we passed Archie's Bridge, and soon after we arrived at the 40th lock at Mullawornia Hill, which marked the end of this long seven-mile level from Draper's Bridge. The lock was in a sorry state, and the lock keeper's cottage was deserted and abandoned. We paused for a while to take a look at the surroundings; the canal along here was built along the side of a very steep hill, with a small lake below us, and a forest in the near distance in the direction of Lough Ree. Both of us had walked the Grand Canal Way in the past, but we were firmly agreed on one thing – the Royal got the best deal when scenery was being handed out. Today's walk in particular, passing as it did along the contour-hugging meandering sections of the canal, was proving to be memorable.

The Flannerys would have stopped and studied the topography around here too. By now they would have spent more than half a day walking along the canal, and would have been starting to understand the engineering involved in canal building. The manner in which the canal clung to the hillside would have left a lasting impression, helping them with their efforts to find riches a few years later during the gold rush in New Zealand's Central Otago region.

The canal builders of old along here probably did not appreciate the lie of the land quite so much as Joe and I did. To them, these hills were a nuisance through which a route had to be driven; the parts that today appear the least interesting to leisure users are the parts that gave them less problems in construction. They suffered a further frustration here; they were a few short miles from Lough Ree and the Shannon here at Mullawornia, but the government insisted that they carry on a further twelve miles north to the agreed river connection point at Cloondara.

From here on we would no longer be walking in a more or less westerly direction, the rest of the day would be spent walking north-westwards towards the canal end. The canal bend around Mullawornia hill forms an elbow on the map of the canal, marking the change of direction of the waterway.

We carried on along the hard gravel road to the old stone arch of Pake Bridge, beyond where the canal ducked under the road again on a new road bridge, swinging hard left as it passed under the span. In contrast to the manner in which the authorities had allowed the canal to decline in previous years, this new bridge was a serious attempt to make up for past sins. It had been constructed with attention to detail, including wooden buffer rails on the concrete walls to prevent damage to boats rounding the tight curve. The bridge had been faced with limestone, which will weather in time to the same mellow patina as the old bridge beside it.

We sat on the wall of the new bridge for a ten-minute break to have a drink and a bit of a rest. We were feeling slightly hungry; the lack of a decent breakfast was taking its toll, but we decided to stick with our earlier plan of making it as far as Island Bridge, still some three miles distant. We had walked eight miles so far, and our lunchtime stop would bring us a little more than half way on our day's trip.

The canal quickly took us away from the road as we left Pake Bridge, and we soon found ourselves back along a grassy path with high hedges and tall trees. The slight breeze we had been experiencing up on Mullawornia Hill was lost to us now, and it was becoming quite warm for walking. Joe was falling a little behind, and I was glad of the break; he had been setting a pace at times over the previous days which I had found hard to match. We strolled the next three miles, taking a good hour to get as far as our target.

We passed Foigha Bridge, the canal twisting around to stay level, creating an attractive environment as it passed a neat house on our left, and soon the good land gave away to bog again. The canal builders hated bog, it was difficult terrain through which to build a canal, but there was no choice here. The only way that they could get from here to Cloondara involved crossing the Corlea Bog. This was not just true in such relatively recent times; recent archaeological work along here has revealed an ancient trackway under the bog, pointing to a route across the swampy ground that dates back to the Iron Age.

The canal skirted the bog as much as possible, but had to cut through a mile or so of it, and we were now on that stretch. It was empty and deserted, with no sign of human habitation in any direction. We puzzled over a large sign which we could see for several hundred yards as we approached it, assuming that the information it carried was on the far side from us. When we passed the sign however we found its reverse to also be blank, giving us something to speculate about as we walked along. Maybe it was an artwork, Joe suggested, and you had to decide your own message to take from it.

The bog was coming to an end as we turned a slight bend and came to a gate that led us on to the Keenagh Road at Island Bridge. The original bridge here was replaced by another bridge that was then replaced by a culvert, as though the local authority was not sure how best to block the canal. We crossed the road and took to the canal bank on the far side, stopping by the somewhat overgrown Mosstown Harbour to have our lunch.

Food never tasted so good, and we offered a toast to Linda of the two name badges for the generous sandwiches. We finished off with a couple of chocolate bars for desert; Joe washed his lunch down with the remains of his water bottle, while I made my usual two cups of tea from the flask of hot water.

Keenagh is almost a mile from here and we resolved to visit it at some future date. The village school was the place where John Keegan Casey, one Ireland's most famous poets, had his first teaching job. Casey is best known for his nationalist poems such as "The rising of the moon" and "The bold rapparee". The poet must have known the canal well; he left the teaching job to work as a clerk in the mills on the River Inny at Tenelick, a place we had passed more than ten miles back.

The harbour here shows promise of being a beautiful place when it has been restored and re-watered. Even in its dry and overgrown state, it is a pretty spot with big trees and beautifully executed stonework on the harbour walls beyond the bridge. This counted as the third road culvert that had still to be removed and replaced with a bridge; we wondered how many more lay ahead before Cloondara.

We were still on the left bank of the canal as we travelled towards the Shannon, now more the west bank than the south bank, due to the change in direction of the waterway since Mullawornia. We still had what we now considered almost a trifling nine miles to go to the canal end, and we were now so confident of completing the trip that we were able to estimate a time at which to meet Pauline in Keenan's bar just across the Shannon in Tarmonbarry. Pauline has adapted so well to living in Connaught that she now only crosses the Shannon when absolutely necessary, hence the choice of meeting place.

We got stiffly to our feet and started to walk along once more. It took a few minutes for us to lose the shuffling gait of two old men, until our muscles loosened and we got back into our stride. We set off along the grassy pathway, lined with high hedges and trees to our left, and with a similar vista on the far side as well. The walk here was sheltered, and we warmed up quickly, soon coming to the next bridge just past the 41st lock at Coolnahinch. The lock house here was in good condition, obviously somebody's home, and a pile of sand pointed to some building repairs being underway. The builder had laid on a temporary supply of mains water to feed the cement mixer; Joe was in luck again and filled his water bottle once more.

Ards Bridge was a mile further on along a good tarmac road; the canal here was still dry, but had enough water lying on its base to encourage a strong growth of reeds. The bridge itself is situated on an open stretch of roadway, and a stiff breeze was by now cooling us down quickly if we paused for a rest. We did not delay here, carrying on quickly past the 42nd lock just downstream of the bridge, and on along the open roadway towards Ballinamore Bridge.

We passed one farm on the left that puzzled us; the access road to the farm crossed a small bridge over a stream which ran on the side of the road, but someone had broken up the bridge so as not to allow any vehicles to pass across it. The farm looked prosperous and well developed, but there appeared to be no one around either the farm-yard or the house. When we got to the bridge the question seemed to be answered; a sign pointed back the way we had come offering a house and farm for sale.

Ballinamore Bridge was a nice stone structure in good condition, but it no longer carried the road; this now crossed the canal on the filled-in bed, the local authority around here was obviously at the leading edge of canal-culverting technology. This brought the tally of culverts still to be removed and replaced with bridges to four so far.

We were back on the canal bank in a very short time; the road we had followed for the past couple of miles diverged away from the canal bank just beyond the bridge. We were now in a sheltered area with thick hedges, a welcome relief from the open ground of the past half hour, when a stiff breeze blew in our faces and slowed our progress. The Crossover Bridge was used in the past to allow the towing horses for the canal branch just ahead to cross the canal and continue towing in the Longford direction. Now it stood forlornly in the middle of nowhere, serving no function but to remind us of how things used to be.

The shelter and reasonably good land gave way quite suddenly to poorer boggy land, and the empty channel of the Longford branch of the canal appeared just across from us on the far bank. This important junction in years gone by was now deserted and empty of people; the present day desolation of this spot gave no hint of the activity that went on here in years past. This was a major junction on one of two main arteries of commerce in the country; the canals carried a huge proportion of the trade and passenger traffic in both directions between Dublin and the hinterland. The long car service from Roscommon met with the canal passage boats here, and many hundreds of almost destitute Irish took the boat from here to catch the emigrant ships from Dublin. In 1845, at the height of the great famine, crowds of more than ten thousand people were often said to have gathered here, as grieving families gathered to bid their farewells to relatives leaving for foreign lands. Now however, we were the only two people to break the silence in this lonely place.

Joe had an idea; this section would soon be restored and re-watered, and this would be his last chance to take a few pictures of the place from an unusual angle. He dropped his rucksack and slid down the steep bank, taking several photographs of the canal from the dry bed. Joe's figure down on the canal bed gave scale to the place; he looked very small down there, and it was more apparent than ever that a considerable amount of material had to be excavated to create this waterway. The canal was wide and deep, and the junction must have been able to accommodate a good number of boats at any one time. The repair crews had been at work here; the canal bed had been cleared and repaired, and looked as though it just needed a lining of clay to be ready for re-watering.

The one thing Joe hadn't reckoned on was getting back up the steep bank. He made a few runs at it but slipped back each time, and my being doubled up with laughter at his predicament was probably not very helpful. Eventually he found a short plank that gave him a foothold, and I was able to reach his hand and haul him back up on to the path.

We carried on again, still on the southwest bank of the dry canal, which twisted and turned slightly, as if the builders had been unsure of which direction to take at times. We soon reached the dry 43rd lock, which seemed to have been more or less repaired, and beyond it Aghnaskea Bridge carried a small minor road over the canal bed. The lock keeper's cottage here seemed to have been restored in the recent past, but appeared empty. An old Ruston Bucyrus dragline excavator lay abandoned on the far bank, "rustin' away" as Joe reminded me.

A short walk took us to the 44th lock and Savage Bridge. Just before the bridge the canal widened slightly to form Kilashee Harbour; the name means "wood of the fairies", as Joe reminded me. The lock keeper's cottage here was in exceptionally good repair, and we stopped to examine a small plaque on the wall of the house beside the front door.

The plaque told us that this was now called Frances' Cottage, named after a now deceased American lady who loved this quiet spot so much that she provided the funds to have the cottage restored to its former glory. The work had been done a few years previously, but local people had respected the restoration job and the cottage was free of vandalism of any kind. Roses grew around the door, a fitting tribute to a thoughtful tourist. Joe photographed the plaque and I am looking at the photograph now as I write.

Frances' Cottage
At Savage Bridge on the Royal Canal
Kilashee County of Longford
Built around 1840 at a cost of 45 Pounds
Restored in 1990

By Frances K. Kelly
Of Forest Hills, New York, U.S.A.
She always loved old buildings and
The history that went with them
Thank you Frances
We love you so and you will always live in our hearts
R.I.P.

We carried on along the same side, the roadway from Kilashee coming closer all the time to the pathway, until both ran side by side as we approached Ballydrum Bridge. A large cleared patch of ground here pointed to what was probably a temporary works depot for repair crews, and the area still had a raw appearance that only time and vegetation will soften. Some stones had been removed or had fallen from the bridge, but these were still on site and restoration would be a simple task.

The road disappeared from view again as the canal drifted away to the right, coming back to join us just before Begnagh Bridge, at the fifth and last major road culvert still to be removed to allow for navigation. Clouds were massing and rain seemed imminent, and we got ready to sprint across the road to shelter under the old stone bridge. An English car stopped beside us, the driver hopelessly lost and looking for directions to Westport in County Mayo, but we were able to point him quickly in the right direction as the heavens opened and we ran past the car for the shelter of the bridge.

The foul weather did not last for long. The rain cleared away almost as quickly as it had arrived, and we hoisted our rucksacks and moved on. Richmond Harbour in Cloondara was now a short one and a half miles away, and we moved along the wide stony roadway with a spring in our steps. Ten or fifteen minutes walking brought us away from the reasonable farmland we had been passing, and back into open bogland that was being worked commercially for the production of milled peat. The canal had been blocked here in a number of places by temporary culverts to allow machinery to cross, but none of these appeared to offer any difficulty with regards to the restoration of the waterway; it would be a simple matter to excavate the fill material and open up the route again.

The surface changed from the new stony road to dry and dusty peat along the next short stretch bringing us to the 45th lock, which was surrounded by a temporary site fence and appeared to be under repair. Such progress was encouraging, although the fence appeared to have been in place for a long time and no work had been done here for several months by the look of things.

The footpath dropped beyond the lock to the bank along the lowest level, and we followed this to a gate that gave us access to a small road leading to Cloondara. Just before Richmond Bridge we left this roadway again and walked along the grassy bank for the last few yards, passing under the bridge and into the harbour area.

Richmond Harbour has been re-watered, and is home to a good many boats of every description. Access from the River Shannon is through a lock at the far end of the harbour, leading to the Camlin River, a tributary of the Shannon. Close to the lock there is a fine dry dock, obviously in regular use, and the harbour appears to be well used and enjoyed by boat owners. A number of people were on board their boats as we passed, and a lot of repair work was being carried out by some of the enthusiasts. As there is no flow of water downstream from the canal, the water in the harbour has to be pumped in from the river, and needs to be topped up every time a boat leaves through the lock. Likewise, the use of the dry dock means that an equivalent amount of water has to be pumped in to replace that lost then the lock is emptied to work on a docked boat. All this will soon change, when water from the summit level makes its way down to here to feed the harbour and the dry dock following the restoration of the final section.

This was another sad place in the nineteenth century when famine and poverty forced millions of our people out of the country. Richmond Harbour was a major embarkation point for of emigrants, with crowds of people gathering to catch the passage boats to Dublin, and many thousands more of their friends and relatives gathering to see them off. For the Flannerys however there was no money for the passage boat fare; they just had to put their heads down and set off along the towpath towards Dublin, another foot-blistering ninety miles away.

We did an about turn at the end of the harbour and walked back to the roadway where it crossed Richmond Bridge, turning right to cross the small bridge over the branch of the Camlin River, and passing by the old distillery. The water wheel that used to power the distillery could still be seen in the disused millrace close to the bridge. This distillery used to be a one of the biggest industries in this area, producing up to seventy thousand gallons of whiskey a year in its heyday, but now but the building was largely unused and not in good repair. However plans were afoot to turn the old distillery into an apartment building.

Passing the old industrial buildings, we were now effectively on an island in the middle of the Camlin, with the cut to the river lock just ahead of us beyond the church and graveyard. The walls of the churchyard were capped with limestone eroded by water, obviously dredged from the riverbed at some stage during the construction of the navigation around here.

Just past the church we crossed a small bridge over the cut, and we spotted a narrow lane leading to our left down by the riverbank. We followed this for a short distance, to where the last lock on the navigation allows boats down to the Shannon. The lock gates here were slightly different from what we had seen on the canal; the racks were operated by a wheel rather than with a rack key, leading us to believe that the operation of the lock here is the job of a full time lock keeper. A hut beside the bank seemed to confirm this view.

We retraced our steps back to the road; a mile of roadway separated us from Keenan's Pub and a good meal. We were still well ahead of the schedule we had given Pauline; we had made good time on the last day. We walked slowly along the road now, not in any great hurry, and we turned left on the busy N5 leading across the Shannon on Tarmonbarry Bridge.

This bridge crosses the wide River Shannon in two steps; the first leg reaches a small island in the midstream; the second bridge with its lifting deck took us across the river and into Connaught.

Keenan's Pub stood out like an oasis on the left hand side of the road, and we settled into comfortable seats and ordered steaks from the menu. Pauline joined us some ten minutes later, and we added another steak to the order. The food, and the obligatory dessert, disappeared quickly, and soon it was time for me to take my leave of my good friends, with Pauline taking Joe home to Newport for a hot bath and a good rest.

8

Tarmonbarry to Strokestown

One word more – for signal token
Whistle up the marching tune,
With your pike upon your shoulder
By the rising of the moon.

The rising of the moon –
John Keegan Casey 1846–1870

I had not yet decided what to do. I had walked twenty-one miles so far, and either Keenan's or the guesthouse next door offered me the possibility of getting a good night's sleep here in the village of Tarmonbarry. I still wanted to get as far as Clooncunny, almost thirty miles away, before taking a break from the walk, but I did not fancy doing all that distance in one day. Neither did I want to walk just the nine miles to Strokestown on the following day, but that town offered the best option of accommodation between here and Clooncunny.

I did have one other option; I could have another cup of tea here and then walk the remaining nine miles to Strokestown. The more I thought about it, the more I wondered if I dared push my body on for another almost three hours on this cold and damp summer evening. The deciding factor was that I did not particularly want to sit around the pub for the rest of the evening, and so I somewhat rashly decided to give it a try.

I almost regretted my decision when I got up to leave; the hour or so I had spent sitting down had allowed all my leg muscles to stiffen up, and both my feet were by now sore and bleeding. Ignoring the looks of a few drinkers at the bar, who must have assumed by my gait that I was suffering from an over indulgence in strong drink, I staggered outside and walked slowly and painfully across the road, walking diagonally between the busy traffic so as to save as much distance as possible.

O'Boyle's Newsagents shop across the road provided me with all the necessary supplies for the journey, and I stocked up on water and chocolate bars, as well as a packet of biscuits. Just beyond the shop, beside a small grotto, a footpath provided a slight shortcut to the minor road to the north, leading away at right angles from the westerly route of the N5 just before a large filling station.

I was soon back to my normal speed, trudging away from the village as the sun started to go down behind the houses to my left. The differences between rural and urban living in modern Ireland were very obvious here; in cities, people on average incomes can aspire to a modest suburban home, while in rural villages the same expenditure can get you a veritable mansion. Each house on this little road seemed to vie with its neighbour for title of grandest home. This did not always mean that the owners got value for money; in the interests of showing off their fine homes to passers by, many of the houses were faced directly towards the road, instead of turning their facades to take advantage of the southerly aspect, but this of course would have meant that their gables would have faced the roadway, which would never do!

With my bag on my back as I trudged along, I felt like an intruder in this landscape, a feeling not helped by the stares I experienced from a Garda who drove slowly past in a very small patrol car. His accusing stare seemed to want me to keep moving and not steal anything, to keep his little patch clean of vagrants and travellers like me. I wondered whether the Flannerys had felt the same; did the landed population around here stare at the four young men as they walked by, willing them to keep going and not stop and frighten the children?

A car repairing business on my right set the only discordant note in this suburban idyll; in order to publicise his place of work the proprietor had somehow managed to park an old yellow van on top of the hedge outside his house, which must have upset his house-proud neighbours no end.

My tired muscles were beginning to loosen up as I walked, and I soon arrived at a point about a mile from Tarmonbarry where the road swung hard left, to carry me parallel to the N5 for the next few miles. The road turned right again, and a minor road ran straight ahead; this minor road was the route I would take. I passed a small dispensary on the left, leading me to idly consider whether I could break in and steal some dressings for my feet, just to give the staring policeman a crime to solve! This is a quiet and pleasant road, although still the location for several mansions which set a slightly discordant note. Two of these now stood on my left; one had a Germanic sounding house name of "Aryan Mist", or maybe the owner was a Van Morrison fan. The next-door neighbour was the police-man, with his little patrol car parked outside.

Beyond this point a sense of normality began to come to the landscape; the houses here were more modest, and a few old houses had been abandoned altogether. One such house had its slates hung in a diamond pattern; I recalled seeing this pattern repeated some-where else, but I could not remember where.

Three miles or so from the village I crossed a narrow gauge bog railway, built to carry out the extracted peat for the power station at Lanesboro. Looking south, I could see the bridge half a mile away carrying the main road over the small railway line, and see the cars passing on the N5 at speed, but even though the wind was blowing from that direction I could hear no traffic noise.

It was starting to rain slightly, but the roadway was bounded for most of the way by high hedges, and there was plenty of shelter. A mile or so later the countryside opened up a bit, with less cover and a lot of swampy land on either side of the road. With the absence of shelter I put on a rain jacket, pulling its hood up to keep the rain off my face. I was feeling tired and miserable, wishing I had stayed in the warmth of the pub, but I trudged on regardless, crossing a little bridge over a small stream.

The road began to climb for what seemed to be a long time, and eventually I crested the hill and stopped outside a derelict house on the left for a drink and a bar of chocolate. Here in the lee of the house the wind was not so unpleasant, and for a while I thought of maybe seeing if the house was open and whether I could have a lie down out of the weather for a while. Before I left the pub I had armed myself with the phone number of the hotel in Strokestown, so I gave them a call to see whether they had any spare rooms. They had a vacancy, so I told them to expect me in a couple of hours. The thought of a nice warm room, and possibly a hot bath, gave me the encouragement to get back on my feet and stop feeling sorry for myself.

I felt that I should be half way to Strokestown by now, but I knew that I had not been making my usual pace and that realistically I might not be quite that far ahead. I kept my head down and carried on. Half a mile on, a big stone house sat close to the road, with a wooden fence all along the roadway beside it. I started counting the posts in the fence as I passed by, then checked myself and put my mind back on the road.

The road had been rising as it passed the house, then shortly afterwards it crested the hill. I half expected to see the church at Scramogue crossroads ahead of me, but the road just seemed to go on for ever in the distance, with another hill a long way off.

At last I found myself cresting the second hill, and I could see the occasional car crossing the road in the far distance. I put my head down again, deliberately not looking ahead for a while, and when I looked up I was close to the crossroads.

I stopped here for a few minutes to consider the rest of the journey. I had by now walked about twenty-seven miles since leaving

Abbeyshrule that morning, and I still had about three miles ahead of me before bed. It was about eight thirty on a cold and wet summer evening, and I was just about finished, not sure if I could even make it the rest of the way to Strokestown. I was still more than twenty miles away from Clooncunny; by this time in their journey the Flannerys would have made it as far as Kilcock. I wondered how they had felt at this point; whether they were as tired as I was at this stage. I doubted if they ever thought of quitting; these were tough young men with a goal, to get out of an Ireland full of poverty and turmoil and get themselves a better life. If they could do it, I thought, so could I. From now on I would put all such negative thoughts out of my head.

Standing here at Scramogue crossroads, I suddenly remembered where I had seen the diamond pattern roofing slates before. Half a mile away to my right there is a small house, now deserted and partly overgrown, close to the roadside. The roof of this house has the same pattern; probably the same builder had a hand in both. I was sorely tempted to walk the mile or so detour to see the house, but I thought better of it.

When the Flannerys walked through here they could never have dreamed that my grandfather Tom, the son of their brother left behind on the farm, would move here to this house many years later with his young wife. My grandmother Teresa was the teacher in Ballyfeeney School close to the house, and their four children, including my mother, were born and raised there. The house did not even exist when the four boys walked past here, and now it is empty and has fallen into disrepair.

I pushed myself forward and moved on, passing the crossroads and the church, and taking the minor road straight ahead down the hill. The road bent left as it dropped down, bringing me back to meet the N5 near the bridge further on. I walked on the hard shoulder of the main road; it was wide and recently built, and the fast moving traffic was irritating after the quietness of the last few miles. I was finding it hard to adjust to walking on roads too; I missed the canal and the way it seemed to keep me company as I walked along. It would have been good to have Joe here as well; when your spirits are flagging a second person can help to keep you moving.

I had made a decision though; I would quit tonight and finish the walk some other time. My feet were very sore, and my body was screaming out for rest. I had nothing to prove to anybody, I told myself, and I could finish this walk anytime.

I stopped by the bridge for a rest, crossing the road to sit in the lee of the bridge wall. I had plenty of water and a packet of biscuits, and I broke these out and ate the lot. I was getting cold sitting on the roadway, and I knew that I would have to get a move on if I ever wanted to get to the hotel. If I had a warmer jacket I could happily have lain down here and slept for a while, but I got stiffly to my feet and picked up my rucksack.

I stumbled the rest of the way into Strokestown, the last mile and a half seeming to go on forever. The safety of the hard shoulder ran out for a brief stretch, and darkness was drawing in, but a line of cones marking the roadworks close to the edge of the roadside provided a safe pathway between them and the verge. The mobile phone in my pocket was clacking annoyingly against some loose change in my pocket, and in my tired and exhausted state I removed the phone and turned the pocket inside out to allow the two or three euro to fall to the ground behind me, putting the phone back in the now empty pocket. The lack of the annoying noise was worth the loss of the few coins, such was the state of mind I was in!

A welcome footpath adjoined the road beside the graveyard on my left, and I wearily trudged along it to where the road bent to the right and the lights of the small town appeared ahead. A few minutes later, thirty miles from Abbeyshrule, I was turning in the front door of the Percy French Hotel and impatiently giving my details to the young man at reception; he had no idea how anxious I was just to get a hot bath and lie down to rest.

Unlike the hotel of the previous night, this place was very pleasant and the room was comfortable, with a welcome bathtub where I could soak my cold and weary limbs for half an hour. I carefully removed the makeshift dressings I had put on that morning; my feet were bloody and sore, and the flesh was so abraded from the tops of some of my toes that I feared that there was nothing covering the bone. I soaked them for some time in hot water, and then left them uncovered while I went to bed and slept like the proverbial log. One thing was sure; I would not be walking very far the following day.

The big man was standing the foot of the bed. "You're thinking of quitting," he said.

"Not thinking of it", I said, "I am quitting. I've had enough of this. You're a better man than I am after all."

"The Flannerys aren't quitters," he said. "There's nothing wrong with you, you just need a bit of food and a sleep."

"But I'm not a Flannery," I said.

"Oh you're one of us all right," he said. "You can't quit now, not when you are nearly there."

"Go away and leave me alone," I said. "Anyway, shouldn't you be gone ahead with the others?"

"I'm just rounding up the stragglers," he said, and he was gone.

9

Strokestown to Clooncunny

I'm a rough and ready fellow
Honest, manly, stout and true
What I love, I love for ever
What I say, I'll always do.

Rough and ready fellow.
John Keegan Casey 1846–1870

I woke the following morning stiff and sore, but otherwise not feeling too bad considering the punishing schedule I had given myself the previous day. Like the dreams I had earlier in the week, the image of Brian Flannery was still vivid in my mind, but I was going to forget about him this time and do the sensible thing; I would take a few days rest to give my body some time to recover.

I dressed the raw flesh on my feet as best I could with the basic first aid material I had in my rucksack, then put on my boots and shuffled down to have breakfast. The service here was very much better than the previous morning, and I managed to put away a good lot of food, even though today I was not going to need as much sustenance as previously. As well as the few guests, the dining room had a scattering of local people enjoying breakfast – a sure sign of a good establishment.

My brother Frank rang me just after breakfast as I was checking out. He knew I was on the road, and he lived less than twenty miles away, so he offered to collect me any time I was ready. I told him I would visit the Strokestown famine museum just down the road from the hotel and that I had no other definite plans, but I would give him a call if I needed a lift anywhere.

I hoisted the bag on my back and walked slowly down the street to Strokestown House and the Famine Museum. This house was the family seat of the Packenham-Mahon family, local landlords at the time of the famine. John Mahon built it in the seventeenth century and it had remained in their hands for several generations, finally being bought in 1979 by a local man who had made his fortune in the motor business. Jim Callery originally intended to purchase the lands in order to allow his business to have room to expand, and to sell off the house and the grounds around it at a later date. However Jim was a local man who knew the significance of the heritage value of the house, and he decided to have it restored at considerable expense, creating a museum and visitor centre to show how people lived in such houses in years gone by.

Jim Callery and his curator Luke Dodd also established Ireland's only museum dedicated to telling the story of Ireland's Great Famine, when millions of our people either died of starvation or emigrated in the terrifying "coffin ships" to other lands, leaving the land to the landlords and the wealthy classes. Our government has never properly commemorated Ireland's Holocaust, practically denying its existence by its neglect, but here in this small town a dedicated individual and his small team have created a moving tribute to all the displaced people of nineteenth century Ireland.

I bought my ticket and wandered around the museum, feeling like someone on holiday now that I had given myself the day off. Any sense of a holiday mood was quickly dissipated however as I absorbed the information in the displays. The full horror of the famine years is brought home to visitors who care to read the poignant notes and letters in the many display cases. Particularly striking are snatches of old copperplate handwriting on scraps of paper, pleadings to the landlord for the chance to work on relief works in order to save children from starvation, as well as pathetic records of workhouse poor and mass burials. These relics of an almost forgotten period reminded me more of the Jewish holocaust museums in European cities than anything else; the parallels in the pictures and records are striking. The manner in which the government of the day and the smug ruling classes were able to blame the problems on the laziness of the starving poor, rather than on injustice and an effective policy of genocide, bears striking resemblances to similar situations today.

One panel caught my eye in particular, its stark figures putting the level of suffering into some kind of context. In 1846 on this estate alone 4,599 evictions were carried out, and the following year 3,000 tenants were forced out. As hunger worsened and arrears piled up, the numbers increased to a staggering 18,000 by 1849. The area of the estate was relatively small in national terms, and the scale of the evictions in relative terms shocked me. It was no surprise to see the details of the shooting of Major Mahon by some of the local people; it was more surprising that people driven to such depths had shown such restraint and not shot more of these cruel landlords.

Jim Callery and his team have done a great service to the country and to humanity in general by collating and exhibiting this material for the education and enlightenment of visitors to Strokestown. Nobody should miss seeing this small museum if they want to understand how Ireland was shaped by recent history, or indeed if they want to get an understanding of the political nature of famines in general. One of the guides in the small gift shop told me that when Jim was going through papers prior to setting up the museum, he came across a letter from one of his own relatives pleading with the landlord for a chance to provide food for his starving children. Strokestown Park museum is a very personal mission for this visionary local citizen, and is all the more truthful and heart rending because of it.

I finished my visit with some tea and scones in the coffee shop, and then shouldered my rucksack again and walked the short distance back to the town. I fingered the phone in my pocket, I could call Frank now and he would be here in half an hour; I could be home that night in my own bed in Maynooth. The train left Boyle about three o'clock I thought, so I could be home about five.

Then again, I thought, what would I be doing sitting around until three o'clock? My feet didn't feel too bad; I could walk a few miles towards Clooncunny, and Frank could meet me on the road in time to get me to the train. I was still reeling from the sadness of the famine museum, and I needed to walk in the fresh air for a while in order to make myself feel better. I was passing the supermarket at this stage, so I wandered in and bought a large sandwich and a few snacks, and the woman at the delicatessen counter filled my flask with boiling water for me.

I was back on the road before I knew what I was doing! I headed up the street out of town, passing the church and taking the Elphin road where the last of the houses marked the boundary between town and country. There was some traffic on the road, but not too much, and it was a pleasant enough walk. About two miles from the edge of town, where a large shed by the roadside houses a tractor repair business, a small road cut off to the left. Glad to be back on minor roads again, I turned off along this side road and headed west.

I was back in real Ireland again. A farmer passing on an ancient tractor saluted me as if I was his closest friend. A couple of cars came along, driving slowly, and the same raised hand of acknowledgement came from the drivers. A mile or so of steady walking and Lough Annaghmore came into view on my left, and I detoured through the car park to take a break at one of the picnic tables by the lakeshore.

I sat down on the wooden bench and ate a bar of chocolate, as well as drinking one of my two bottles of water. I had not bothered to carry my usual stock; I had figured that I would not need so much for a short walk today. Now however I was beginning to revise my plans a bit; I called Frank and told him that I would call him back in the afternoon. I might be able to walk half way to Clooncunny today, and leave just a short walk for another time to finish the journey.

I rejoined the road at the end of the car park, passing a minor road on the left, and later on a large modern house with stone eagles on the gateposts. Beyond the house the road was obviously less used, with grass growing along the centre. I like a road with a green median; it means that very little traffic passes the way and that it is ideal for walking in safety and quietness.

About a mile away I reached the small crossroads and turned right, heading north again. The road here ran through bog, and the surface rippled and twisted where the road base constantly subsides. A few people were working on the bog, and ricks of saved turf were stacked by the roadside here and there, ready for hauling home.

The road crossed a small stream and passed a minor road on the left, then began to rise. As it rose the land lost its peaty nature and became more fertile; the small hill I was now climbing must have been an island once in the lake that is now the bog, and would have been the scene of human habitation for a long time.

I came to a sort of staggered crossroads, with a small road to the right and a road to the left about twenty yards further on. The road I was on crossed a small river on a pretty three-arched stone bridge; beyond the bridge I took the road to the left and walked on around a slow bend. The central median here was grassy also, and I relaxed again and just enjoyed the walk.

This pleasant country road meandered a bit and rose slightly, taking me along between small farms and high hedges, with several houses along the way. I approached one such house where a noisy dog barked at my approach, and a large sign warned me to beware of the dog and to enter at my own risk. The owner was standing outside, looking at the sky; an elderly man approached on an ancient black bicycle, freewheeling down the slight hill towards the house. A few yards before the house he partly dismounted, throwing his leg over the bar with surprising agility for a man of his age, and cruised to a stop before the other man, dismounting finally with a few quick dainty steps to come to a halt in front of the house.

"Howya Mickey", said the man who was looking at the sky.

"Howya Mickey", said the cyclist. The dog that guarded the house here had to deal with having two Mickeys it seemed.

"What'll it do Mickey?" said the house owner, whose gaze had returned to the sky.

"I'm in doubt it'll come wet," said Mickey two.

"Have ye much hay down Mickey?" said Mickey one.

"None yet Mickey", said Mickey two.

"We'll have to make bleddy silo Mickey"

"We will Mickey, bleddy silo".

I walked on and the rest of the conversation faded behind me; I wasn't the only one wondering if rain was on the way.

The road emerged on to the main Roscommon to Sligo road and I turned right; the busy traffic raced past here but I only intended to stay on this road for a few minutes. I crossed over to the far side and walked the hundred yards or so to the crossroads, turning left again along the R369. A tap on the wall of the cemetery caught my eye, and I filled the empty water bottle. I drank the remainder of the second bottle and refilled it as well, no harm in being prepared. I made a mental note to tell Joe that every cemetery in Roscommon seemed to have a water tap on its wall; in my tired state the night before I had noticed a water tap near the gate of the cemetery on the approach road to Strokestown. While it might look as though the local authority was providing water for all of its dead voters, I figured that these taps were put there to allow people to clean up gravestones and to water the flowers.

Just past the cemetery I turned right again, following a signpost for Ballinameen. A mile down this minor road I stopped in the lee of a concrete cattle pen and sat down for a while to have some more water and another bar of chocolate. I debated whether to eat the sandwich and drink the tea, but I was going well and I decided to keep these in reserve; I was now toying with the idea that I might try to finish the walk to Clooncunny after all. My feet were still sore but were not getting any worse, and I really wanted to emulate the Flannerys' trip if at all possible.

As usual, getting to my feet was difficult, and I walked stiffly for a few hundred yards until I got loosened up again. I was feeling cold from sitting down, but soon warmed up again with the exercise. The countryside around here was familiar; born and raised not ten miles distant, I had often driven along this way, but this road had never seemed quite so long in the past. The farmland beside the roadway was poor, bordering on boggy in places, and where farms had been neglected they were quickly reverting to rushes and scrubland. The few well managed farms stood out greenly in the landscape; places like these will probably be less and less common in future years when agricultural policy moves away from subsidised over-production to a completely market-led system.

A fine house and tidy yard on my right was no longer a working farmyard, but a depot for the trucks of a transport company. The rain was close now, starting to spit a little, so I stopped and put on my rain jacket in the lee of a lone ash tree a little farther on. A mile or so on I stopped to take off the jacket again; the rain had been threatening all morning but now seemed to have changed its mind and the sky was brightening in the west. Where the sun broke through the cloud it was warm and pleasant. The road was quiet, with few houses, and one attractive home stood on my left just ahead. As I passed by the house the front door crashed open and a young boy came charging out. He couldn't have been more than two or three years old, but he was sturdy and full of life. "Where you live? Where you live?" he yelled at me.

His mother, a pretty young woman ran out and grabbed at him in embarrassment. "Come in here Jack" she said, "the man is just going for a walk". She apologized profusely to me, but I was not offended. I told the boy that I lived nowhere, just walked the roads all day, and that that was what would happen to him if he didn't go to school.

It was good to see people returning to this area to live; I remembered it as a place scarred by emigration, with houses closing up as the remaining few elderly bachelor farmers died off. Now it seemed that young families were returning to repopulate these houses, bringing life to this rural community again. A house on the right was being rebuilt too, and was surrounded by a site fence worthy of any city building site. The fence was plastered with site safety signs; nobody without a helmet and safety shoes, as well as a high visibility vest and a safe-pass card, would get to enter this haven of safe work practice.

The reality of course was that this was not the city but was rural Ireland. Two young men operated a concrete mixer, dressed in old tee shirts and jeans, with not a helmet in sight. The heavy safety shoes were not evident either; both lads were wearing runners as they worked.

The road beyond the house was narrow, and made narrower by the way in which the hedge on my side had grown out on the road, forcing me to walk near the centre. A white car approached at speed, towing a small trailer of turf, and I pressed in against the hedge as tightly as I could to give him room to pass. The driver's face was set; bringing home the turf is a serious business and he was a man on a mission. A loose sod of hard black turf fell from the trailer just before he drew level with me, and it bounced along the road like a ricocheting bullet, catching me hard on the ankle as I tried to jump out of the way.

The leg gave way under me with the sharp pain, making me fear that I had broken my ankle, and I went down on one knee, rubbing the injured spot for several minutes until the pain began to subside. The white car was speeding away, the driver unaware that he had done any damage. I rolled down my sock and examined the blackened bruise, with the skin just broken and oozing blood. It didn't look too bad apart from the bruise, and as the pain eased I stood up carefully and tried it out to see if it would bear my weight. Thankfully there appeared to be no permanent damage and I hobbled on towards Ballinameen. A mile or so later, only a dull ache reminded me of the incident.

A sign for "Ballinameen community alert" gave me hope that the village might be close, but I crested one hill, and then another, with no sign of the elusive place. I could see a wind farm in the far distance to my left and I knew it to be situated on the hills above Monasteraden, a few miles past my eventual destination. It was too far away to be able to count the windmills with any degree of certainty, but I was cheered somewhat that my target was at last in sight.

Finally I crossed a rise and the church spire came into view on the right hand side of the road. A small development of new houses was being built behind the church; I was more than a little surprised at this kind of progress in this small place, but it was good to see that Ballinameen is now seen as a desirable place to live, and not as in the past when it was somewhere to leave as soon as you were old enough to emigrate.

I stopped at the village store and post office to stock up again on snacks. I walked in the front door and spotted my old friend John, the owner, standing by the counter. He was surprised to see me carrying the rucksack, and asked me where I had come from.

"From Dublin'" I said.

"Walking?" he asked incredulously.

"Yes" I said, "I walked all the way". I had not thought about that until now, my mind more on where I was going than where I had been. Now that John had asked the question, I was a bit surprised myself at the fact that I had walked 120 miles in just five and a half days.

John also runs a taxi service, and he offered to drop me anywhere I wanted to go. I politely refused his offer. How could he understand that nothing was going to stop me now until I got to where I was going, now just eight miles away? I said my goodbyes and left the small shop, turning the corner and taking the road for Boyle.

The old national school on the left was built in 1879. In my day it was the parish hall, used for occasional dances and for the Christmas fundraising bazaar. Now it has been practically rebuilt by local voluntary labour as a community centre, and a plaque told me that the Irish President had officially opened the centre in 1999.

A mile or so further on I passed the GAA football pitch, following the pleasant winding road with only an occasional car passing to break the silence. This was one of only three Gaelic pitches along the route, including Croke Park. The GAA, now the largest sporting association in Ireland, did not exist when the four Flannerys passed here; it was founded many years later in 1884. A sign on a house on the left advertised "Boyle Stained Glass", and just beyond this house I arrived at the small crossroads that is known locally as "Granny Cross".

The road to Boyle turned to the right here, and a small road turned left towards the bog. The other small road, more or less straight ahead, was where I needed to go. This road is narrow and quiet, and after about a hundred yards I stopped beside a ruined house to have my tea and sandwich. I spread my rain jacket on the ground and sat down; I was hungry now and I made short work of the food and drink. When I had finished eating I lay down on the jacket and put my rucksack under my head for a pillow, and I was soon fast asleep.

I must have slept for an hour on this warm afternoon, lying there on the grass verge. I would probably have slept for longer had my phone not roused me. My brother Tom was calling me from his home in America; I had told him I was going to walk across Ireland. "Where are you now?" he asked. I told him that I was on the road near Granny Cross and that he had just woken me from a sound sleep by the roadside. "Let me get this straight" he said, "You're sleeping in the gutter in Ballinameen, right?" I agreed that that was more or less the case. "I always knew you'd turn out bad," he said.

I packed everything back in the rucksack and got to my feet, shuffling along the narrow winding road for a while until I began to find second gear. This road used to be almost bereft of human habitation in latter years, although in my childhood I remembered a thriving community living around here. Now, although several houses were still unoccupied, there were signs that the area was being revitalized, with houses being renovated and modernised.

The road ended at a junction with the main road from Boyle to Frenchpark; I was now in County Sligo, getting ever closer to my destination. I turned left along this road for a while, towards Frenchpark, and a couple of hundred yards on I turned right again down a narrow lane heading west towards Lough Gara. This road again has a friendly green median, and no cars passed me all the time I walked along it. The weather had turned for the worse again, with cold squally showers making walking unpleasant; I sheltered from one heavy shower in a small calf shed in a field close to the road.

The road turned hard left for a while, ignoring an old grassed-over road that ran straight ahead. It headed up a steep hill after the bend, and a hundred yards further on it took a hard right turn, running again in a westward direction. The road appeared to have been diverted in the past to avoid wet ground lower down, taking to the higher dry ground on the hill.

On the top of this hill I saw a sight that cheered me no end; I could see Lough Gara shining in the distance, the sinking sun in the west reflecting off the water like a silver mirror. The lake has two parts, Upper and Lower Lough Gara, and a short river runs between the two lakes. The bridge across the river is at Clooncunny, and the Flannerys were born in a little house just beyond the bridge.

The fact that I could now see the lake made me reflect once more on the journey made by my relatives as they walked through here on the way to Dublin. I still could not help but think in terms of their being on the road at the same time as me, albeit going in the opposite direction. Irrational as it seemed, I was now conscious that they would be somewhere around Cabra, with the Dublin city sky-line very much in view. They must have been cheered at having reached their first destination, with the long walk almost over. I was feeling much the same, able now to see the target of my almost six-day walk just ahead, not more than half an hour away.

This must have been the place where the four Flannerys had stopped to look back at Clooncunny for the last time. It is said that they stopped at the top of a hill and looked back once at the lake, and then never looked back again after that; this had to be the place. I could imagine how it might have been; some of the local lads would have accompanied them part of the way, and then turned near here and went home leaving just the four boys to carry on. If they had looked back at Clooncunny and their returning friends it might have been too much to take; their hearts must have been breaking at the thought that this was the last time they would ever see their home by the lakeshore.

As a schoolboy I cycled this road every Sunday in the summers, going from my home to fish at the bridge. I knew every house on the road, as well as every bend and feature. In my day this road was not even tarred, it was just a dusty link road with a high grassy median that only local people knew about.

The road wound around slightly, heading all the time more or less westward, with occasional slight glimpses of the lake in the distance. It dipped down through some poor land and then climbed again, passing Drury's house just before it joined a slightly wider road at a tee junction. Members of the Drury family in my time were local celebrities; one of their cousins was James Drury, the Hollywood screen actor and star of "The Virginian", a long running western series on TV when I was young. We had to take people's word for how good James Drury was of course; none of us had a television set in those years.

I turned left at the junction, and then right a few yards away to head west again towards the lake. Ten minutes walking brought the lake into view on the right hand side of the road, with the bridge away in the distance. Lough Gara was drained in the 1950s when the Boyle River was deepened, and the lowering of the water level in the lake revealed a large number of Crannogs, the lake dwellings of early Ireland. Some of these artificial islands showed signs of habitation for millennia, and a number of archaeologists have spent a lot of time excavating and quantifying the artefacts revealed by the lowering of the water level.

I walked to the bridge and stopped for a while, leaning over the rail to stare down at the brown water below. I spent many happy days here leaning over this rail; this place was a gathering point for dozens of people on sunny summer Sundays in the 1950s and 1960s. Old and young gathered here on Sunday afternoons to try their luck at coaxing a few perch from the rushing river. Not for them the carloads of equipment favoured by modern day anglers; the tackle of choice for most was a small wooden frame on which a coloured hand-line was wound, terminating in a yard of clear nylon line and a single hook. A float consisted of a cork drilled through with a nail reddened in the fire, and a feather quill was jammed in the hole through which the line was threaded. By removing the feather quill, the cork could be slid up or down in the line to vary the depth of the sink. A single earthworm, or sometimes a leatherjacket grub, was baited on the hook. Some of the less organized fellows didn't bother to even dig for worms, relying on cadging a few from other people on the bridge.

It would be standing room only all along the rail once the afternoon arrived. A few people who got there earlier got the best spots; there were a few places in the lee of the bridge abutments where the fish were easier to catch. Harry Conry always got there first, and I would be there soon after, and we would talk and fish all day. The others arrived one by one, depending on how far away they lived or how late they dined, and soon the bridge would be at once a fishing party and a political debating chamber. I was never conscious of it at the time, but many of the people who lined the bridge were related to me in one way or another; this was Flannery country.

The Flannery family survived the famine in part because they could supplement their diet with fish from the lake, and the tradition of fishing was strong around these parts. When I fished here as a youth it was a continuance of this tradition; we caught a few perch or maybe a pike in season, and the fish made it to the frying pan the next morning. There was never any notion of fishing just for the sport of it; there was always the underlying notion that we were out on the bridge looking for tomorrow's breakfast.

I was beginning to feel the cold, so I moved on, over the bridge and west along the road towards Monasteraden. The old schoolhouse stood abandoned just beyond the bridge; it was beginning to deteriorate and become overgrown. The stone above the door dated the building as having been built in the 1880s; it did not even exist when the boys left home.

I was getting to the end of my journey, and despite my tiredness I quickened my step. I passed another house, and then a tidy hedge came into view on the right hand side of the road. A neat new bungalow stood behind the hedge, and a wide gateway gave access to the house and the yard behind it. In the yard, still intact after all the intervening years, stood the original home of the Flannerys; my cousin Paddy built the new house a few years back but preserved the old home. When some of our relations came back from New Zealand to Ireland in the 1980s they were able to sit at the fire in the old house – a fire that was said not to have gone out over well more than a century since the four Flannerys left home to seek their fortunes.

I walked up to the front of the new house and knocked on the door, but there was no one at home. Paddy must have been out somewhere, and for a minute I felt a sense of needing to leave a message, but then I remembered that that had been just a dream. I walked around to the old house and put my hand on the door to mark the end of this part of my journey, and then I turned and walked back towards the bridge. I paused for a minute to lean over the five-bar gate and look at the old hedge that had divided the Casey farm between Brigid and Una; the significance of such landmarks is almost lost nowadays.

I called Frank and asked him to pick me up, and he promised to be along shortly. I was tired and sore; the miracle fabric that made up my boots was designed to "wick" away moisture from my feet, but an ominous dark stain on the top of the boot made me think that it was now wicking away some of the blood from my left foot. I dreaded finding out the condition of my feet when the boots came off.

Eugene called me; my friend is a marathon runner and knew I was out walking, and he was wondering how I was getting on. "Have you managed to avoid getting blisters?" he asked.

"Funny you should ask" I replied.

"You should be using Vaseline," he said. "You rub it between the toes every morning and it stops the friction that causes the blisters".

That was just what I needed to know, but a week earlier!

I waited at the bridge for my lift, walking down by the lakeshore to sit on a bench and have a drink of water. A dark cloud was moving in, and a sudden shower forced me to run for the cover of the bridge. As I sheltered from the rain I noticed a small plaque fixed to the wall with a short verse engraved on it; other places have graffiti, but Clooncunny has poetry. There was no credit given to the author, but the words seemed to fit the location.

> *Light on shadowed bed*
> *Perch and eel dart silently*
> *Seeking unmapped stones.*

10

Chatto Creek to Matakanui

I knew the stars, the flowers and the birds
The grey and wintry sides of many glens,
And but half remember human words,
In converse with the mountains, moors and fens.

Nature's child – J.M. Synge 1871–1909

The four Flannerys and Tom Donnelly stood on the hill above Tinkers. They had staked a claim on this expanse of mountainside, the only claim left in the Otago goldfields. Nobody else wanted the mining rights to this stretch of hillside; there was no point in owning a claim when you couldn't get the gold out. A man called Murphy had previously staked it, and the claim's official name on the map was "Murphy and party", but now it belonged to the four Flannerys and the Englishman.

Further down the valley there was frantic activity in the various claims. Anywhere there was enough water to wash away the gravel there was a mine of some sort. Tom Donnelly had worked for wages for the previous two years on the Blue Duck Mine, and he had made a bit of money. More importantly, he had learned the skills that would be needed if they were ever to get this gold out of the ground. The Flannerys had saved a fair amount of money too; they had been careful with the wages they had earned in the last couple of years, and had a good stake to get them started here in Central Otago.

There was gold in the claim right enough. They had spent the previous two weeks digging a series of trial holes on the claim, and the assay of the deepest gravel layer showed the presence of some gold at least. There wasn't a hope of getting it out however without a lot of water, and the claim was too high up the hillside for any of the rivers or creeks to provide a stream of water to wash away the gravel. In any case, no matter what river or stream you looked at, some miner already had a claim to its water, and there was no chance of any of them giving up those water rights.

The water had to be available in sufficient volume and at sufficient height above the claim to provide the head pressure needed to wash away a layer of gravel up to a hundred feet thick from more than a hundred acres of mountainside. The way it appeared to everybody who had looked at this claim up to now, there was no way on earth that this could be done.

Tom Donnelly and the Flannerys had other ideas. They knew that there was a supply of water at Chatto Creek that could be diverted to operate the mine; there was enough volume and it might just be possible to bring it to a height to give the head pressure that was required. There was only one problem; Chatto Creek was not far away as the crow flies, but the nature of the terrain meant that the water would have to be diverted for more than twenty miles.

"It's very simple", said Brian Flannery, "we just need to dig a canal that is twenty or so miles long, and keep her level, or just enough slope to give us a flow. If we lose height on the way, even a little bit every mile, we will bring the water in too low and it won't work". "Still", he said, "it's only digging, and we are well able for that".

Tom Donnelly was also enthusiastic; he knew that this could be done. "I know how to get the gold out" he said; "If you lads help me to bring in the water, we can get enough gold out of this claim to make us all rich".

"Enough talk so", said Brian Flannery. "Are we all in for this, win or lose?"

His three brothers exchanged glances, and nodded.

"I'm with you boys," said Donnelly. "We'll do it so".

The small team set to work straight away; Donnelly worked out the height of the point above the claim that the water would have to arrive at in order to provide the correct pressure, and they added another twenty feet for good measure. From this point on the hill they then set off with a long spirit level, sighting along it for as far as they could see in the direction of Chatto Creek. Two of them would go ahead with a bundle of pegs and a sledge hammer, and the two men with the level would call out to the peg-man to bring the peg up or down to a point that was at the same level as the man doing the sighting-in. The two forward men moved on, and the two behind walked as far as the peg and sighted ahead again. In this crude manner they surveyed a level line to where they proposed to divert water from the creek and send it along the side of the mountain to their mine.

There appeared to be enough water in the creek at this point for their needs, and it was still early in the summer when water levels were fairly low. If the creek could give them a plentiful supply of water at this time of year, there would surely be more than enough come wintertime.

The next thing they needed to do was work out how long it would take them to dig the canal; the mine was only ten miles from the creek as the crow flies, but the water race would have to zigzag in and out of the hills to maintain a level, and the overall length would be well more than 20 miles. They dug the first section for a full day and measured up; by dividing the amount they had done into their estimate of the total distance they figured that it would take them two years to get the water to Matakanui.

That created a problem. Even by pooling all their money, they did not have anything like enough to see them through two years of work. They needed tools and equipment, and enough food for the team for two years. They decided to talk to Gilbert Sinclair.

Sinclair was something of a legend around the goldfields of Central Otago. He ran a general store in the town of Blacks, the place that has nowadays reverted to its original native name of Ophir. He made his living selling supplies to the miners and the mine owners, and he was often paid in gold for his goods. In the days before banking had become established in the area, he also acted as a banker of sorts, often staking men who owned claims until they could bring in the gold and pay him back. He was a well-liked and respected man, and the Flannerys and Tom Donnelly approached him and told him of their plan to build a canal from Chatto Creek to Matakanui.

This was a bit different from the normal request for a month or two's credit for a miner working a claim; in this case he would have to wait at least a couple of years for his money, and if the boys gave up or failed in their marathon digging session he would not see a penny of his loan back. It was the most audacious scheme he had ever heard of, to operate what was reputed to be the one unworkable claim in the valley, but Sinclair was a good judge of character. He decided to take a chance on these young men, and the deal was sealed with a handshake. As soon as their own money ran out, he would provide the credit for all the supplies that they needed.

This might seem an unusual way of doing business, but Gilbert Sinclair was an unusual man. He had no great interest in wealth, and he had a great liking and respect for the mining community. Many years later, when he knew he was dying, several of his relatives called to see him, hoping to inherit the debts owed by a lot of the miners in the area. Sinclair had other ideas; he called his lawyer and together they burned all his account books. His legacy to many a struggling miner in Central Otago was a clean balance sheet; he took the debts with him to the grave.

It seems simple in the telling now, but this was an enormous undertaking by any standards. The five men had only a basic education, and none had the skills of an engineer or a surveyor. All they had were good heads on their shoulders, and a determination born of poverty and deprivation that made them very keen to make a go of this endeavour. In addition, they had no way of knowing whether the claim would yield enough gold to make the whole effort pay; there was a vein of gold-bearing gravel running along the mountain-side, but it was possible that this had thinned out or disappeared altogether where it ran under their claim. The whole operation was fraught with risk, but that did not deter these men.

"We came to this country with nothing", Brian Flannery was often heard to say, "and the worst thing that could happen would be that we have nothing at the end of this". On the other hand, they knew that this was their one big chance to make it, a once in a lifetime shot that might never come their way again.

They set to work on the digging. Some of the early stretch was easy enough, just digging a wide channel and building up the banks with the material they had excavated. They had just one crude piece of equipment to keep the bed of the channel level; an isosceles triangle of timber with a base made from a long straight-edge about eight or nine feet long. A plum bob hung from the apex of the triangle, and when the point of the plum bob hung down to meet a small saw cut on the middle of the base, the straight edge was level. They would use this instrument to check each section of the bed of the race, alternately turning it around in the opposite direction to compensate for any errors that there might be in the way in which it had been assembled.

The summer was getting warm and the work was hard, but all the men were tough and resilient and they kept going, working full days from first light to dusk. By the end of the first year they had moved ten miles along the side of the mountain, working through the winter in the snow and the severe frost that hits this part of the country. By this time their own money had run out and they had begun to draw supplies from Gilbert Sinclair.

The second summer saw a very dry spell, and they worked on; they were ahead of schedule on the distance, but they had underestimated the total of extra digging that was required to get the line in and out of every gully and spur along the mountainside. The summer gave way to winter, and still they dug their canal, living where they worked in a crude hut made of sods and built into the side of the hill. Every so often they demolished their bothy and rebuilt it nearer to the work, moving house along the side of the Dunstan Mountains and digging from morning till night. From Ophir, Sinclair could mark their progress by the smoke of their campfires and by the thin level line that could just be discerned along the side of the hills. A few people teased him that his money was gone, but he smiled and said nothing. He had the measure of these boys.

By the end of the second year the canal was supposed to have been almost complete, but all had not gone to plan and they were still six months or more away from the target. The terrain had proved worse than expected in some places, with a lot of rock and hard ground, sometimes bringing progress down to a couple of yards a day. In addition, they had to get around the side of some very steep hills, and this necessitated building up the race by carrying in loose boulders from a wide area. The one thing that never crossed anybody's mind was the notion of quitting; the Flannerys were not the quitting type.

Eventually, the race arrived at the header area for the sluicing, and all that remained was to let in the water. First they had to make up a number of aqueducts to carry the race over various creeks that they had crossed along the route. These they made from thick wooden planks, stopped up with heavy clay, and in a matter of days this was done and the water began to flow.

It is reckoned that betting men all along the valley lost a lot of money that year. The claim had been written off as impossible by almost everybody, and the Flannerys and Donnelly were generally considered to be a little crazy for their audacious attempt to divert Chatto Creek all the way to Matakanui. Only Gilbert Sinclair was seen to be smiling a little more broadly than usual as he collected his bets.

The rest, as they say, is history. The water ran strong through the sluicing guns at the claim of "Murphy and party", now officially renamed as "The Undaunted Gold Mining Company". The crew worked for several months more, washing away a section of the top layer of overburden and then the gold-bearing gravel below. The first "wash-up", or extraction wash, yielded enough money to pay Sinclair, and Brian Flannery and Tom Donnelly set off for Ophir to settle the debt. To their surprise however, Sinclair handed back the gold.

"Keep it for a while more" he said, "you will need working capital to get the operation moving, and I can wait a few months more for my money"

"You know it is safe now anyway", said Brian.

"I always knew it was safe", said Sinclair.

He was right too. The mine went on to be one of the most successful in New Zealand, and the company was eventually floated on the London stock exchange. It produced a lot of gold and made rich men of the Flannerys and Tom Donnelly, but it didn't change them much.

Brian Flannery went on to farm a huge swath of the Ida Valley, just across the hills from Ophir, and even to this day that land is in the hands of the Flannery clan. Tom Flannery bought another huge section in the same valley, and this too is still farmed by the descendants of the miners. Michael took his share of the money and moved to Auckland, where he joined the prison service, eventually retiring as Governor of the Eden jail in that city. Peter stayed on to help manage the Undaunted Mine, and ended his days in Matakanui, down the hill from the end of the canal he helped to build.

11

Clooncunny to Charlestown

And I must walk the road that winds
'Twixt bog and bog, while east there lies
A city with its men and books
And treasures open to the wise.
Heart-words from equals, comrade looks;
Down here they have but tale and song
They talk repeal the whole night long

A poor scholar of the forties –
Padraig Colum 1881–1972

It was a couple of weeks before I got a chance to go walking again. My feet had mended well and almost no sign of the blistering could be seen. On a sunny morning I parked my car beside the wind farm on Largan hill and Frank collected me and dropped me outside Flannery's house in Clooncunny. Paddy Flannery was again away somewhere, so I put on my rucksack and started to walk westwards towards Monasteraden. The road was quiet, with few cars, and the morning was bright and seemed to foretell a fine day. Hay was saved in many of the fields along the road, and here and there some healthy looking potato crops interspersed the hayfields. The land leading down to the lake is dark and peaty, but is known to grow good potatoes, and most households grow enough for their own use.

The potato is still important in Ireland; even today most Irish people do not consider that they have had a proper main meal unless it includes potatoes. In the early part of the 19th century the potato was the basic foodstuff that kept the population alive. It was eaten boiled with the main meal of the day, or boiled and mixed with a little flour to make potato cake, or grated raw with flour and a seasoning of salt to make boxty. The failure of part of the crop over several years of the early part of the century, and the almost total failure in the 1840s, created the famine that resulted in the death or emigration of millions of people. Even when the worst shortages were over in the latter part of the century, the tide of emigration carried on. Young people saw little point in staying in a country where starvation was never far away, and where there was little hope of ever having a stake in the country that was firmly controlled by a foreign power and the local landed gentry.

While the emigration of the four Flannerys to New Zealand did not happen as a direct result of the famine, there is no doubt that the famine created the conditions whereby they felt that they had little other choice. These few fields here beside the road might provide a living for one family, if you were happy with a basic subsistence living, but all the Flannery boys could not live on these few boggy acres. There was no choice but to leave, taking the road away to the east and never coming back.

It was one of those mornings when it is good to be alive. The day was fine and sunny, but it was cool enough for walking at a good pace without feeling overheated. I was making good time and I had soon passed Lomcloon and reached the outskirts of Monasteraden, passing the former Island Road railway station. This branch line used to run from Kilfree Junction on the Dublin-Sligo line, to connect with the larger town of Ballaghadereen a little to the southwest of here. The Kilfree line was built a couple of years after the main line, and it went the way of many such branch lines, closing down for good in 1962.

You can still see where the line ran, although the tracks are overgrown. The former station house on the right hand side of the road is now a private dwelling, but the platform has by some miracle survived, along with its capping edge of large cut stone slabs. My grandfather Tom left from here when he went to Belfast to join the police force; by then people were still leaving to find opportunity in other places, but the fortunes of the Flannerys had improved since his uncles walked out the front door and turned left for Dublin. Tom had turned right and had enough money in his pocket to catch the train.

I was walking along at a good pace, keeping one eye on the road, when I spotted the glint of coins on the roadside. I stopped and gathered the handful of loose change that lay scattered by the road-way, about three euros in all. It seemed that the road was giving back the money I had dropped when I struggled to make the last mile to Strokestown, more than twenty miles back. Later that evening a charity collection box on a shop counter seemed to stare accusingly at me; I dropped the money in the box and felt better.

There is another Flannery story from here that is worthy of mention. In 1881 Joseph Corcoran and one Brian Flannery, the latter probably a distant relation of my granduncles, were shot dead near here by a police party who were attending at an eviction on behalf of Major Arthur French, a local landlord. A tenant family had fallen behind with their rent and Flannery and Corcoran were among a crowd trying to prevent the eviction from taking place. The process server fired his revolver into the crowd, killing Brian Flannery, and Constable Armstrong fired his rifle and killed Joseph Corcoran.

The enraged crowd turned on the police party with sticks and stones and killed Armstrong, and were about to stone the injured Constable Hayes to death when a local woman called Mary Bermingham took pity on him and shielded him with her body. When Hayes later recovered from his wounds he proposed marriage to Mary Bermingham and she accepted. The eviction papers were never served and the eviction never took place. A monument erected in 1956 marks the spot where the two men were killed, and people around here still speak of the killing as though it happened within living memory.

I crossed the road at Monasteraden and took the narrow lane straight ahead up the hill, quickly gaining height until I could look back at the lake and the little village. Climbing further, I turned and saw the entire area of the upper and lower lakes was spread out behind me, making sense of the map that I unfolded as I took a break for a drink in the hot sunshine.

The road continued on for the next four miles, like a roller coaster up and down steep hills. Since I had left Dublin, largely helped by the route finding skills of the canal builders, I had largely avoided hills of any kind. Now however I seemed to be making up for the easy walk so far; the road now seemed to be throwing everything it had at me to try to slow me down and tire me out.

This area is attractive, but has suffered its share of dereliction caused by poverty and emigration. A number of fine houses were empty and abandoned, with the shrubbery and undergrowth taking over and trying to pull the buildings down. A few were finding a new lease of life where young people had made a return to the countryside, trying to live the good life in this beautiful place. There were even a couple of new houses along the road, offering hope that this area will eventually revert to being the thriving community it once was.

The road took a final dive and then a steep rise, and I joined the slightly busier R293 that links Gurteen and Ballaghadereen. I turned left towards Ballaghadereen, keeping well in on the right of this well surfaced road as a few cars passed at high speed.

I could see the wind farm on Largan Hill very clearly now, the cluster of nine huge windmills with their rotors turning lazily in the slight breeze. They really dominated the skyline along here, and when I had walked a mile or so I could hear their blades cut through the air as they turned.

Just beyond the wind farm, where the road I was on curved off to the left, I took to the side roads again, turning right up the hill. This was a quiet narrow road, with a few houses near where it left the main road, and with one house very near the swishing wind-mills. A little further on I stopped at the gate leading to the wind farm, where I had parked my car earlier. I had walked a mere ten miles, not wanting to overdo it on my still tender feet, but I felt good and ready for more in the morning.

I had company again for the next leg of my journey, the eleven-mile stretch as far as Charlestown. My niece Lisa from Boston, as well as her friend from school, Leah Donovan, were in Ireland on holiday and were already bored. A walk through the countryside would be just the thing to pass a day, and would be something to talk about when they got back to school in Boston in the autumn.

We didn't start too early; American teenagers, like their Irish counterparts can be hard to get out of bed in the morning. Eventually we set off, having first poked around the wind farm to see the giant turbines up close. We crested the hill and moved off at a fast pace down towards the forest and the bog on the far side, but within about ten minutes my two companions were already lagging behind and I had to slow down to wait for them.

A road joined us from the left at the forest, and we carried on, through the next crossroads at Boleysillagh and the next again at Brogher. The pace was very erratic, with sudden spurts and then protracted spells of slow walking and looking at every little detail of plant and insect we passed.

This is beautiful countryside, wild bogland with views in the distance towards Ballaghadereen, with the spire of its church clearly visible in the distance. Ireland has many of these beautiful small roads, often as here almost parallel to the main road but with almost no traffic to spoil the walk. The two girls were taking pleasure in the freedom of this day as well, and were enjoying each new discovery as they poked in the hedges as they passed. An old white bath was in use as a drinking trough for cattle in a gateway; we had to stop while I used their camera to take a picture of both of them squeezed into the bath.

The road descended towards Derinacarta crossroads; the two girls, walking behind, were startled when three young men sped past them on racing bikes. We passed the church and the crossroads, and the three lads were standing with more of their friends outside a house, eyeing up the two girls as they passed. My two usually cool American pals were suddenly red-faced as they walked past the boys.

"Did we give ye a fright?" asked one of the lads.

There was silence from the two girls, as they walked scarlet faced past the gauntlet of young men. A hundred yards later they had regained their composure and were mimicking the young men's flat accents perfectly. "Did we give ye a fright?" Said Lisa, in an accent that was pure Sligo!

We stayed on the same road for another six miles, passing through a mixture of poor land and the occasional cluster of green and well-tended fields. Signs of life returning here were evident too; there were still a few closed-up houses, but others were being repaired and a few new houses were appearing. This is the part of the world made famous by the late John Healy in his book "Nineteen Acres", where he highlighted the death of communities as emigration decimated whole parishes. "No one shouted stop" he said; nobody listened to him much either, and the rot continued for a long time afterwards.

We were walking more or less parallel to the main road, the N5, and gradually our little road came closer and closer to the busy highway and we could hear the noise of the heavy traffic off to our left. A short while after passing through the small crossroads at Lissymulgee we joined the N5 at an acute angle, crossing the busy thoroughfare quickly and carefully to continue on up the little laneway on the far side.

The last mile or so had been slow; I was approaching mutiny in the ranks if we didn't have a rest stop soon. The old handball alley stood a short distance away, partly falling down now and unused, and we found ourselves a few stones for seats and got out the sandwiches.

The girls had been reluctant to make a lot of sandwiches that morning, but now they would have eaten the wrappers, such was the appetite they had built up with their walk in the fresh air. They demolished their sandwiches and drank all of the water they were carrying, but I had anticipated a need and had packed a box of muesli bars and extra water. I opened the box of snacks and these quickly went the way of the sandwiches.

"It would be cool," said Leah, "if loads of people started to walk this route. We could open a café here and sell them all coffee"

"And muesli bars" said Lisa.

"We could call it the LLJ café," said Leah, "after our initials"

"Lets call it that anyway," said Lisa. "We're having lunch at the LLJ café."

I walked back this way a year or so later and was a bit shocked to find that in order to provide access for machinery and equipment used in constructing a new road, the authorities had demolished the handball alley. It was like losing and old friend, and when I called Lisa and told her I could hear the disappointment in her voice. "That's the end of the LLJ cafe," she sad sadly.

The next half-mile was taken up with discussions on the LLJ café, until an ancient tractor with a transport box on the rear passed us by slowly.

"It would be cool," said Leah, "to take a trip on the back of a tractor all along these little roads"

"Yeah," said Lisa. "We could organize tractor holidays."

At least, I thought, they were far from being bored with the afternoon's walk. They were looking at everything as they passed, taking pictures of butterflies and flowers. Some of the blackberries were turning prematurely ripe, and we picked these and ate them as we walked along. The girls were amazed that you could get "loads of free stuff" in the hedges, and at first they were concerned that it might not be good to eat. They soon got over any reservations, and before long their hands and lips were stained purple from the plump blackberries.

They were falling behind again, and I stopped by the roadside to wait for them. A well-trodden patch of grass by the bank caught my eye, and I went to investigate. The path led to a spring well in a field on the right, and the water looked clean and clear. I took the cup from my flask and drank a few mouthfuls; the water was cold and tasty, good spring water is hard to beat on a summer day.

The girls were fascinated; they had never seen such a thing. "It's mineral water," I said, "non-sparkling."

They looked at me to see if I was having them on, but eventually they decided to try drinking from the well. They drank their fill and filled their water bottles with the delicious water. "Wow," said Leah, "you could live for free here."

"Yeah," said Lisa, ever the practical one. "You wouldn't sell much water in a café around here."

The road weaved left and right, between tall hedges in places, with the air full of the scent of wild flowers and with birds singing everywhere. This stretch of road is very peaceful, and only an occasional car or tractor passed slowly along to disturb the peace. Just beyond a piece of forest we arrived at a quiet crossroads, with a road running away to the right at an acute angle. This road, I knew, could take us to Charlestown, but would involve walking on the busy N5 for more than a mile and without the safety of a hard shoulder. Instead we went straight ahead towards Puntabeg.

The road now began to twist and turn, but was opening up again with views over surrounding fields. Two tourists on bicycles came along in the other direction, with map bags on their handlebars, cycling slowly and enjoying the countryside. It is amazing that very few tourists ever venture on these lovely side roads; there is a treasure of beauty and tranquillity just waiting for anyone who gets even slightly off the beaten track in the west of Ireland.

There were horses in a couple of the fields along the next stretch, around Puntabeg. This delayed us again; my two pals had to coax the horses up to the fence and offer them bunches of grass plucked from the verge. The horses were not impressed; they looked well fed and the fields were full of lush grass.

We eventually arrived at the crossroads at Bracklagh, and turned right here along a road that was just slightly busier. A religious shrine by the side of the road was another object of curiosity. "What's it for exactly?" asked Leah, puzzled at the elaborate glazed temple around the plaster statue. Another photograph of the two girls beside the shrine heralded the end of the roll of film.

About a mile from the crossroads we arrived at the main N17 leading into Charlestown. There was nothing of interest to dally about here, and we all picked up pace and walked quickly along the hard shoulder over the last mile to the town. A filling station and shop on the outskirts provided ice cream and a stop for bathrooms, and we were soon in the centre of Charlestown where I had dropped my car earlier in the day.

We were only about five minutes outside the town on our way home when I glanced back to the back seat; Leah was fast asleep, stretched out with her face squashed in the contents of a packet of crisps. She slept like that for the rest of the journey; eleven miles in the country air was too much for this city girl.

Lisa chatted all the way home in the front seat. She had enjoyed the day and was ready for more, but then Lisa is made of sterner stuff. After all, she is twenty five percent Flannery!

12

Charlestown to Pontoon

And all along the quiet town
We marched right stern and slowly
Until we stood among the dead
In silence calm and holy

We laid our baby martyr down
We strewed his grave with flowers
Where longest lingers heaven's light
In heavenly summer hours

Dirge – John Keegan Casey 1846–1870

I had decided to wait to finish the walk to the coast until Joe had walked from Tarmonbarry to Charlestown; the plan was that we would finish the last forty miles together. That was what we intended, but then both our lives got busier and busier and before we knew it summer had turned to autumn and then to winter and we hadn't got around to finishing what we started. I was determined to complete the walk before the year ended, so I put aside a weekend in late November and headed for the west of Ireland one Thursday night, with the intention of making an early start on Friday morning. The days were now very short, with darkness falling early and making for unsafe road walking in the evenings. I needed to get to Pontoon by about four thirty in the evening in order to complete the walk in safety.

I found a hotel in Knock in County Mayo. Knock is a small village whose main industry is based around religious worship. Religion is big business here; most people staying in the hotels and guesthouses are here to pray at the shrine, a kind of Irish Mecca for Catholics. My fellow guests in the hotel appeared to be serious worshippers; there was none of the jollity over breakfast that you would expect in other places where people went for a weekend break. I resolved to find somewhere else the following night. After a reasonably decent breakfast I drove the few miles to Charlestown and parked the car, getting on the road around nine o'clock in the morning.

There were few people about, but the supermarket in the square was open and had a well-stocked delicatessen counter where they made up some sandwiches for me. I had already filled my flask with hot water from the kettle in the hotel bedroom, so I stuffed the rucksack with the food and a few snack bars and set off out of town along the Swinford Road. A few hundred yards on, past the filling station, a small laneway turned right by a house with a white-painted garden wall that was perforated by small concrete balusters. The road looked as if it might be leading to somebody's back yard, but I had studied the map and I figured that it would take me where I wanted to go.

Half a mile from the corner the little road I was on crossed the old railway line, now overgrown and with the sleepers rotting away and the rails rusting. There is pressure now from the people of the west of Ireland to re-open this line, but it will take a lot of money and effort; all that really remains of this infrastructure now is the right of way.

The road turned sharp left just beyond the railway, and ran through a sleepy little backwater with just a few houses scattered around. Another half mile of walking brought me to what looked to the casual observer like a dead end, with the surface deteriorating and high grass growing in the middle of the road. Trees and bushes grew high on each side, closing over above my head to form a tunnel that must be cool and shady in summer.

There were a few dilapidated houses along here, and my slow walking pace gave me a chance to look these over in a way that would not be possible if I were to be driving past. Each house, when viewed from a walker's perspective, told a story of someone's attempt to wrest a living from this mediocre land in this albeit beautiful place. One particular house stood solid but abandoned on the right, with a little decaying barn on the other side of the road; I could picture a farmer strolling across to milk his cows on a winter morning like this, before returning to the warmth of a good fire. It was sad to see these small homesteads abandoned in this way.

The road dipped down and then rose again, re-crossing the railway and ending at a T-junction. I turned right here, past a couple of houses and some abandoned shipping containers, and the road began to emerge from the high hedgerows into open countryside once more.

A small road veered off to the left, but I kept to the right hand branch, heading northwest and crossing the railway again. I was now in poor land, with a lot of bog and forestry plantations to my right hand side, and the road was empty of cars and people. The morning was cool but fine and the rain seemed to be far away for now.

A woman came towards me, walking her dog, but she did not respond to my greeting and walked by as if I did not exist. I found this to be unusual on my travels, as most people would at least speak in a friendly manner, and quite often would want to know where you had come from and where you were going.

The road branched up ahead, with a rough limestone block set into the ground at the fork in the road, and the name "Lislaughna" carved on one polished face of the stone. This is a recent phenomenon in rural Ireland, where community groups erect stone signs with place names on them. I welcome this development, even if many of the stones look like markings on a tomb; the sense of pride in place that causes these markers to be erected at some cost and a lot of trouble is to be applauded.

I knew I had to take the right branch at Lislaughna, in spite of my instincts that told me that my destination was off to my left somewhat. I was taking a curving diversion from the main road, sticking to these tiny roads away from traffic and noise, where I could enjoy the sheer pleasure of walking down the middle of the road with the wind in my face.

The land around here is poor, so much so that it is hard to imagine how people managed to feed themselves and their families in the days before EU farm subsidies gave small farmers a decent standard of living. It is easy to understand how people here just gave up and caught the emigrant boats to a better life, right up to recent times; I could see from the small fields and boggy ground how it could just all become too much. You could farm this place for twenty years, getting nowhere, and one day you would face the inevitable and turn the key in the door and leave. John Healy sounded the alarm bells about the death of a community, but successive governments either did not know what to do or did not care, and only membership of Europe and a booming economy has managed to bring cash to these poor places.

Twenty minutes of brisk walking brought me to a T-junction, with a slightly wider road running off to my left and to my right. I turned left, heading more or less in a westerly direction, past some prosperous looking houses and an industrial yard. An occasional car passed on this stretch, but it was not exactly a busy highway and made for pleasant walking.

A small building on the left hand side of the road caught my eye as I strolled along. At first I took it to be a water pump-house serving some of the houses on the right, and I wondered that a mains supply had not reached this area. As I came closer however I realized that it had been built to house a small shrine, and had been finished off to keep the plaster statue warm and dry behind a modern pvc-framed window. The shrine was labelled "Cloonfinish 1996", a reference to the townland I was now passing through. Religion had become very high-tech in this area; the shrine we had passed on the approach to Charlestown when I walked with Lisa and Leah was not in the same league at all.

About a mile further on a small road turned right, just before another old handball alley. These alleys are dotted all around Ireland, built by local voluntary effort in the years before people had money in their pockets to spend on leisure pursuits. People would gather at the ball alleys in the summer evenings after a hard day's work in the fields, and would compete in hard-fought games of handball. Now these structures are mostly falling down; nobody nowadays would do something so simple as play a game of handball in their spare time. This one has been luckier than most, unlike the LLJ café; the local community has made progress in restoring the alley here and are working to revive the sport of handball.

The road was quiet again, and twisted around a bit as it approached the big bridge over the River Moy at Ballanacurra. A small road peeled away to my right for Cloonainra, but I kept straight on, guided by the large-scale ordnance survey map that was proving very necessary around here. I stopped at the bridge for a drink of water, dropping my rucksack by the roadside to rest my shoulders. Having cooled my thirst I strolled over to the bridge rail to look down at the rushing brown water below, leaning well over the rail to see if I could spot a salmon making its way upstream.

A small car passed, and then came to a sudden stop just as it crossed the span, pulling in quickly at a parking place at the end of the bridge. A middle aged woman got out of the car and walked across towards me; I acknowledged her presence and went back to staring at the rushing river; she approached me and asked me if I was all right. I was puzzled at her query; surely I didn't look like someone who needed assistance?

With a shock I realised why she had stopped; she thought I was about to throw myself over the rail. I must have been stretching over the side to look directly down when she passed, and she jumped to the wrong conclusion.

I turned to look at the woman; she was dressed in a severe looking tweed coat with a pioneer pin prominently displayed, and looked as if everything in life was a serious matter to her. "God gives us life", she said, "and only God can take it away."

On the one hand I thought that she meant well, having obviously thought that she could save a soul from the sin of suicide, but the temptation was too much for me. I looked over the rail again; "it's lovely down there," I said. "The fishes are in out of the weather, don't you think?"

She looked alarmed, not knowing whether to grab me or start a prayer; I felt a bit guilty at winding her up and I walked back to my rucksack. "Time to be on the road" I said.

The woman got back in her car and drove slowly away, looking back to make sure I didn't change my mind. I walked on towards Foxford with a lingering feeling of guilt at the way in which I had pulled the leg of an obviously sincere person, albeit someone who was prepared to see problems where none existed.

The road ran on, through better land now, passing straight on through the small crossroads at Dromada Gore, or so another limestone marker informed me. A further mile away another stone told me that the road to the right went to Killasser, but I didn't want to go to Killasser and I kept straight on. The land was alternating between middling and boggy, and the drains and small streams by the roadside were loud with rushing water. The sky was now leaden, and the rain was beginning to spit a little, giving promise of some heavy stuff very soon.

A small shop and post office stood on the left, set back a bit from the road, and I made note of it for another time. At the moment however I was still well stocked with supplies, and I had no need of a shop. There was a telephone kiosk outside the shop too; something I would have thought was almost obsolete in rural Ireland nowadays, when most people own a mobile phone. It was good to see it surviving though; too many rural post offices are closing and leaving older people without facilities in these remote areas.

Another stone stood on the road, where it turned hard left, telling me of the location of Blackpatch. A tidy house stood at the bend of the road, covered in creeper, and a small road turned off to the right by the side of the house. I had almost missed this turn, it looks as if it is someone's driveway, but I turned right along it, and then immediately left again on an even smaller road. A sign pointed to a heritage centre, but other than that it almost felt as if I were trespassing here; the middle of the road was grassy and it looked to be little used.

I crossed a small bridge over a little rushing stream, and then passed a side road to the left with a sign for the heritage centre. I was a bit disappointed; my route took me straight ahead and I would have liked to visit the centre if it was on my way, as much to get out of the impending rain for a while as to see what was on offer.

I was on part of the way-marked Foxford Way here, with the posts and their little walking man insignia visible here and there in the bushes by the side of the road. I had to run the gauntlet of a house with about half a dozen very unfriendly Alsatians throwing themselves against a chain link fence as I passed. The rain was beginning to fall steadily now, and I started to look for some shelter by the roadside.

There was none to be seen just yet. I crossed a slightly wider road at Graffy, and a couple of hundred yards ahead I spotted a shed just off the roadside, with the gable door invitingly open. I crossed the gate and made a dash for the shelter; the rain was now beating down furiously and I would have been soaked in minutes if I had remained on the road.

I took stock of my surroundings; the shed had obviously once been a school or a large house, and had at some later stage graduated to housing cattle. Now it was empty except for a few old plastic and steel stacking chairs; I dusted off two of these to make a picnic area, and got my flask and sandwiches out of the rucksack. A couple of cups of tea and two sandwiches later, the day was beginning to look better, although the rain was still drumming down, finding all the weak spots in the roof, but leaving me dry.

Half an hour later the worst of the rain was over, and it had settled down to a steady drizzle that looked to be down for the day. I was beginning to feel a chill too, the day was not too cold but I needed to keep moving to stay warm. I packed up my bag and put on my rain gear, and crossed the gate to get back on my journey.

The road ran downhill again, picking up another road that joined me at an angle from the right. I dropped further down, then the road rose sharply again at a right hand bend and I walked through the little hamlet of Cullin. This place was built on the high ground on the side of the hill, up out of the boggy land below me to the right, and had the look of an idyllic village in days past, but now it was almost deserted. Fuchsia hedges surrounded the little cottages, but now only one of the old houses and one new house showed signs of habitation.

The road bent back left as it left the village, dropping down as I passed the last of the houses. I stopped and had a drink of water to mark the spot; I had reached the edge of my second last map and one more ordnance survey sheet would take me to my destination at Newport. I felt a sense of being on the home straight, that it was almost all downhill from here.

The dark bulk of Larganmore Hill rose steeply to the right of the road; this was the first piece of mountain scenery I had encountered on my trip. With a few minor exceptions the route I had chosen across Ireland was never too hilly or taxing, and was proving to be a delightful trip, even on a wet day like this. There was water everywhere, with small drains and dykes carrying noisy streams away to the Yellow River and on towards the Moy.

The road made a left turn at Collegrane Shrine, beside the Tempall Maol cemetery, and I went in to have a look at some of the old gravestones. This graveyard had been here for a long time, with a mixture of relatively modern headstones and some old famine standing stones. The place had been cleaned up by local effort, and a stone plaque told of the history of the place.

This memorial stone is dedicated to the memory of all burials in this cemetery, in marked and unmarked graves, including victims of the famine and black flu, not forgetting all the babies buried here, baptized and unbaptised.

The stone was dated 2002, and I thought that it was a kind and respectful effort by the local community to have taken such care of this place. I felt moved by the thought that so many famine victims had perished here; it was easy to imagine that people would have died here by the thousand in this inhospitable land when their staple diet of potatoes was lost to them by the blight that ravaged the crops in the middle of the nineteenth century.

I am always conscious that we are the survivors of the great famine. So many of our people died of hunger at the hands of a largely uncaring colonial power, and half the population either died or left the country for good. The Flannerys lived through the famine itself, but by the time that they had grown to manhood the tide of emigration was running at full ebb and they were carried away with it, on a one-way trip to find a better life in a country far away.

Back on the road, the rain had started to come down again, not too heavy but persistent and enough to make the day miserable again. A big minibus pulled up the slope from the side road and turned the corner by the cemetery wall; the driver looked me up and down, trying to decide if I was out for a walk or if I needed a lift away from the weather. I motioned to her that I was ok, and she smiled and drove on, no doubt wondering at the type of idiot who would choose to get a voluntary soaking on a wet winter's day.

The road carried on, crossing a slightly more important road and winding its way through a landscape scarred by worked-out gravel pits. Just over two miles of damp walking brought me back to the N26, heading left to Swinford and right to Foxford. The junction was within the boundaries of the latter town; I turned right and a few minutes walking brought me to the town centre. I paused at the memorial to Admiral William Brown on the left hand side of the street. This Foxford native who lived from 1777 to 1857 was the founder of the Argentinean Navy and is national hero in Argentina.

A quirky antique shop on the other side of the road invited exploration at some future date, and beyond it the William Brown Memorial Hall told of the pride of this town in its native son. I walked straight on at the crossroads and crossed the River Moy for the second time that day; it had now picked up a lot of extra water from various tributaries and was flowing in full spate under the town bridge. The road to the left was signposted for Pontoon and I headed west along that way; the sign told me that I had only 4 kilometres to go. It was a quarter to three, and the rain seemed to have finally stopped for the day.

The road to Pontoon crossed the railway just outside the town, and then passed through a wooded section before Lough Cullin began to shine through gaps in the trees. The lake had a small beach and picnic area beside the road, and I stopped for a rest and a drink, peeling off my clammy rain gear and consigning it to my rucksack.

A couple of hundred yards further on I joined the road from Ballina to Pontoon, and I turned left towards the latter. Lough Conn lapped up as far as the road on my right; I was now on a narrow spit of land that separated it from Lough Cullin, with the tiny village of Pontoon situated just before the bridge that spanned the channel between the two lakes. The hotel seemed to be closed for renovations, and was surrounded by a builder's hoarding, so I decided to carry on to Healy's, a couple of miles further on, for some food.

Mentally I had targeted the village as the end of my walk for the day, and I found the further two miles or so to be heavy going. Half an hour later, with darkness starting to fall, I gratefully pushed my way in the front door of Healy's bar and guesthouse, which commands one of the most attractive views in Ireland, looking south across the calm water of Lough Cullin.

I took a seat in the dining room and ordered some food; I was cold and hungry and I was grateful for the warmth of the cosy restaurant. I stretched back in my chair and a sudden soaking rewarded me; water was dripping from an ominous bulge in the ceiling. I called over the waitress and showed her the problem; a flurry of activity ensued with staff running around in panic. It transpired that a guest in one of the upstairs rooms had used the shower with the door open, flooding the floor and the ceiling of the dining room. Eventually calm was restored and a nice meal was delivered to my new table, well away from the still dripping spot on the ceiling.

Over desert I asked the waitress if she could order a taxi for me; I wanted to go back to Charlestown and pick up my car. She brought a list of the local taxi companies and their phone numbers to the table and I picked the last one on the list; I figured that the ones at the top of the list would probably get the lion's share of the business.

The woman who answered my call said that she could certainly bring me to Charlestown, and that she would be with me in ten minutes. I finished my meal and moved outside, and true to her word the big minibus U-turned into the car park just as I emerged from the building.

I climbed into the front of the bus and did a double take; for a moment I could not remember where I had seen the driver before, but then I realized that she had passed me at the famine graveyard at Tempall Maol earlier in the day. She realised at almost the same time where she had seen me earlier, and we immediately got into a conversation about my travels across Ireland.

Margaret proved to be a great choice of taxi driver; she had a wealth of local information and stories and was a skilled and safe driver on these wet and twisting roads. I hoped that I had enough money to pay for the trip; I had just thirty-five euro in my pocket, and I estimated that thirty-euro should cover the fare, leaving five euro for a tip. The conversation helped shorten the journey, and soon we had arrived in Charlestown. I got out and pulled my bag from the bus.

"How much do I owe you?" I said, fingering the notes in my pocket.

"That'll be thirty five euro," said Margaret.

I handed over the money; there was nothing left for a tip. I thought of Joe's witty answer to the tipping dilemma.

"Never run with your laces open," I said.

She was still looking at me with a puzzled expression as I closed the door and headed for my parked car.

13

Pontoon to Newport

Oh, I would we could wander while the blue stars glimmer
Through the gracious salmons' abode;
Oh to quietly wander where the fruitful hazels
Bear each unripe load
Above the rocks by the blue lake waters –
Lovers wandering down by the waters
On a shining sandy road.

Drummin Wood – F.R. Higgins 1896–1941

Healy's restaurant and guesthouse was cosy and the rooms were comfortable, and I slept soundly. The breakfast was plentiful, but I was not in the mood for the usual fry. Instead I asked the waitress if she might put the sausages and rashers in a sandwich to take with me. She readily agreed and brought it to me wrapped in tinfoil; I was somewhat surprised however to find a sandwich added to my bill when I checked out.

I left the guesthouse and turned right, up a steep hill on the Crossmolina road. Two attractive and solid stone houses stood on the left hand side of the road, with wonderful views over the lake. One of these, I knew was once the RIC barracks, commanding this important vantage point where the road crossed between the two lakes, and I recalled that the other might once have been a hotel. A pity it still didn't offer bed and breakfast I thought; a bit of competition wouldn't go amiss around here.

The Foxford Trail soon joined me from the right; this route had looped around the back of the hill behind Healy's guesthouse, skirting the shore of Lough Conn. I had originally planned to take this route had I stopped at the hotel in Pontoon for the night; it is one of the more scenic routes in Ireland and gets the walker off the road for most of its length. Still, the traffic had not been a problem anywhere I had walked to date, and these country roads were safe for walking as long as I finished each day's walk in daylight.

The road wound around a bit and went up and down hill, but the morning was pleasant for walking and the surroundings were lush and attractive. Here and there on my right I could catch glimpses of Lough Conn where its inlets came close to the road. There were quite a few houses around here too, some of them located in very pretty places indeed. Not for the first time since I had set out from Dublin, I was passing through a place that seemed to provide an exceptional quality of life for its inhabitants, with the mountains at their backs and the lake at their feet.

One such pretty spot gave a great view of the lake as it came right up to the road, and beyond it a laurel hedge and a small gate lodge indicated the existence of an old retreat of the landed gentry. The style of the lodge pointed to grand living from another time, when the wealthy landlords lived in some comfort amid the squalor endured by their tenant farmers. The hard conditions endured by the natives in this area in the years following the famine helped to breed a tough resilient people who were able to stand up for themselves. Not far south of here, on the estate of Lord Erne near Cong, Captain Boycott retired from the army in 1880 to become the land agent for the estate. The Captain proved to be so cruel and severe that the tenant farmers and all the tradesmen and women of the district shunned him, bringing his name forever into the language as a term for social and commercial exclusion.

A small break in the hedge and a set of well maintained steps pointed to the presence of another spring well, and I stopped to check it out. The water looked clean enough, but it was too close to the road for my liking; the rainbow colours of some spilled petrol ran too near the verge and I decided to give this well a miss. Still, if the day was hot enough and I was thirsty enough, it was good to know that a good well could be found here.

Just beyond the well I left the main road and turned left, up a small road following a sign that said "Lake Levally, Pike" I followed the road uphill for a while, and then crested a rise to see the grey expanse of Lake Levally spread out on the left hand side of the road. The wind was blowing up the lake from the south, bringing large waves crashing on the stony beach along the roadside, and depositing a beard of froth and dead reed stems along the shoreline. The pike would be safe enough today.

A field beside the lake had four donkeys in residence, and they were evidently pleased to see me if that was what I could interpret from their frantic braying that continued long after I had passed by the end of the lake. Levally, like Lough Gara, is another lake that has the remains of a number of ancient lake dwellings or Crannogs, and there is reputed to be one close to the road here, but the waves and wind-blown spray today made any sight of it impossible.

A sharp left hand bend brought the road across a bridge over the small but fast running Derrinurchers River, carrying water from the lake on to its bigger cousin Conn. The wind pushing the water up the lake today was obviously helping to swell the little river, which was running very fast and looked dangerous; in summertime I had stopped here to look over the bridge at the trickling stream in this idyllic spot, but it was hard to remember today what it had looked like then.

The road set off up hill again. I could now see the bulk of the mountains ahead of me, with Nephin dominating the skyline just ahead on my right. I was now in mountain country, and Nephin looked dark and inhospitable on this winter's day. I had climbed to its summit in the past, and the view from the top is rewarding, but it is bleak place in the winter months.

Still climbing, the road came to an end at a T-junction, with a signpost that pointed to the left towards Newport. I turned right however; I had a different route in mind. I wanted to get completely off the beaten track on this last day of my trip, and I knew just the road for that. A hundred yards on I took a left turn down a small laneway; this little road looked like it might end at the house a little way in from the main road, but I knew that the small bog road led on across the hills by Bofeenaun. This would be my last chance for a while to walk in one of the most dramatic landscapes in Ireland that can be enjoyed without taking to the hills. It is one of the most scenic roads in the country and you rarely meet a car on it.

A dog barked as I passed the house, and he watched me carefully to make sure I kept on walking. A farmer was feeding sheep by a gateway a little further on, but unusually he ignored my greeting in a rather rude manner. There had been some run-ins between landowners and hikers around here, both sides determined to rub the other up the wrong way, and that might have explained his antipathy to a walker with a rucksack on his back. Either way, I wasn't going to let his rudeness spoil my good mood; I was coming in sight of my goal of walking across Ireland and nothing was going to spoil my day.

I stopped for a short break at the small lake called Lough More a couple of miles further on. A flat stone surrounded by furze bushes gave me a place to sit and get some shelter from the sharp breeze, and I drank some water and chewed on a snack bar. I decided to call Joe to see if he was home; I would be passing his house in a couple of hours and it would be nice to have him walk the last few miles to Westport with me.

Joe was out in North Mayo with a group of young students from his school, but he assured me that he would be home before I got there. I told him where I was sitting and he gave me some background information on the location – his local knowledge and his historian's skills were the things that made him an invaluable travelling companion in this part of the world. This little lake, seeming so insignificant to a passer by, is of immense importance in archaeological terms. The diggings just across the road from me, which I had assumed were the traces of a local farmer's turf cutting work, were in fact the remains of an extensive archaeological dig that had been carried out some years previously. The dig had uncovered evidence of an important settlement here in the Iron Age, with fuel from the bog having been used to smelt iron ore from the hills in a crude furnace.

I needed to get on; the day was chilly and did not allow me to sit for too long. I hefted the rucksack on my back again and set off along this quiet but beautiful road. It can be busy enough here in summertime, with farmers cutting and saving turf in the bog, but now in mid winter it was deserted. I had this dramatic landscape all to myself, with no cars or people to break the silence. In the distance I could see the bulk of the Nephin Beg range of mountains, almost dead straight ahead. The wind was hard in my face at this stage, tearing at me and pushing me back, so that I had to put a lot of effort into each step, but it was exhilarating nonetheless and I knew that it would ease off when I got down lower into the valley at Glenhest.

I checked my watch; it was just after eleven o'clock and I figured that I was about eight miles out from Pontoon. At this rate I would be in Newport in good time; I had still about ten miles to go, but it was mostly downhill or on the flat from here. The road surface had changed from tarmac to gravel at some stage but I had not noticed the transition; the tarmac had been so badly potholed and broken up that when it ran out I had not been aware of any change underfoot.

Eventually the road began to drop down to meet the R312 from Crossmolina to Castlebar. I crossed this road carefully; the howling wind made it difficult to hear cars approaching. The Newport road ran straight ahead, and was more sheltered and well surfaced. A sign at the crossroads advised me that Newport lay 14 kilometres ahead, just short of 9 miles I reckoned.

The road crossed the Crumpaun River just beyond the crossroads; the bridge, with its nice low walls looked like a perfect place to sit and fish on a better day, but today the water poured brown and fast through the arches, looking dangerous and uninviting. The road began to climb slightly again, and as I topped the hill I could see the large bulk of Beltra Lake shining in the valley to my left. A short time later I turned off the road into the car park of the community centre and found a place to sit out of the wind; it was time for lunch.

My breakfast sandwich looked a bit congealed and not too appetising, but it tasted a lot better than it looked and I wolfed it down with a couple of cups of tea from the flask. It was not a day for lingering, so I quickly packed away the wrappings and moved on. The sign nearby said 10 kilometres; Newport, and the Atlantic Ocean were now firmly in my sights.

Glenhest is a nice place to live. Some attractive new houses looked like expensive designer homes, but I found out later that the local authority had built them for its tenants. It is good to see such an enlightened attitude to housing design among local bureaucrats; for too long such a scheme would have been made as unappealing as possible; now they had managed to create some very desirable homes on a relatively small budget.

Frank Chambers, the local auctioneer, was selling a very boggy site on the right, according to the colourful sign that was nailed to a post. It looked like a most unlikely place to put a house, but the builders in this part of the world are well used to the vagaries of bad ground and can build houses that never subside or crack in the middle of the bog. The secret, as Joe often tells me, is in digging down to "the solid", as it is called here. The blanket bog is not very deep here, and an excavation of ten feet or so will often find perfectly sound footing for a house on a site that looks impossible to an outsider.

The monument on the right marked the site of an ambush in 1921, when the West Mayo IRA brigade under Michael McGiolla Ruaidh fought the British forces. Joe's house stood a few hundred yards ahead, and I was soon sitting in his kitchen for a welcome bowl of soup.

We left together for the final few miles to Newport. Joe did not have the disadvantage of having walked all day, and he was fresh and able to set the pace, while I struggled to keep up. We passed along the road by the forest, until the bog again gave way to better farmland and the houses became more plentiful. There were plenty of signs of prosperity here; the houses were all nicely appointed and had well laid out gardens and boundary walls. Unlike the Mayo of famine times, the people of this area now enjoyed, if anything, a better standard of living than their city relatives. The good times had come to Mayo, and looked set to stay.

The scattering of houses started to thicken up, and the countryside began to merge into town. We passed the school and the road from Achill and Mulranny, and walked on up the town. The buildings on the right had been derelict for as long as I could remember, but now a crane swung overhead and a small army of builders swarmed over the site; even Newport was in the grip of a building boom. The awkward bad bend at the top of the main street remained however; Joe told me that the planners had decided to have it retained, since it was part of the essential character of the street, and the news cheered me. Too often, quirky streetscapes like this that have evolved over centuries, are straightened and sanitised in the name of progress; here the decision to keep to the original line of the street seemed to make so much more sense.

We marched down the main street, moving quickly now and eager to get to the end of the road. I was glad that Joe was with me to share the end of the journey; he had been with me at the beginning, when I set out to emulate the journey of the four Flannerys, and it seemed fitting that he was here now.

We crossed the bridge over the tidal estuary of the Newport River. To our left the sandstone arches of the railway viaduct glowed pink in the evening sun; the bridge is the defining landmark in this little town, but the trains no longer run here. Like much of the infrastructure that was inherited from the colonial power, successive governments chose to throw out the baby with the bathwater in the rush to cleanse the country of all English influences. What need would we have of railways anyway, since the policy for decades was to export our people and depopulate the west of Ireland? The money the emigrants sent home would be enough to give the old and the very young that remained the power to buy the few protected goods made by the well-connected rich, allowing the country to be run for the benefit of the few. As happens in so many places, the people of Ireland swapped one form of tyranny for another, and opportunists within the new political system quickly filled the void left by the departing power.

We turned by the end of the bridge along the south quay, our fast walk petering out into a stroll as we realized that this was more or less as far as we wanted to go. Short of walking down to the line of the ebb tide across the mud and seaweed, we were now at the end of the road. Pauline was waiting to collect us, and she used my camera to take our photos as we leaned against the quay wall. A few passers-by stared from their cars at this well dressed woman taking a photograph of two scruffy middle aged hikers on this sunny winters evening, wondering no doubt at the reason for it all.

We climbed into Pauline's car and headed for Pontoon. This part of my journey was over.

14

The Famous Flannerys

There's gold, and it's haunting and haunting;
It's luring me on as of old;
Yet it isn't the gold that I'm wanting
As much as just finding the gold.
It's the great, big, broad land 'way up yonder,
It's the forests where silence has lease;
It's the beauty that fills me with wonder,
It's the stillness that fills me with peace

Spell of the Yukon – Robert Service 1874–1958

The small alarm clock buzzed annoyingly; it took me a minute to figure out where it was in the strange room, with the early dawn light barely peeping through the curtains. Christina pulled the duvet over her head and told me to be quiet; like me, she had not been able to get much sleep the previous night with the racket from next door. A gang of travelling sheepshearers was renting the house across the way, and they had been having one of their noisy parties well into the night. The police had called around midnight and told them to turn the stereo down, and they had complied until the police car had turned the corner, when the racket had immediately started up again.

I had seen the stereo silhouetted against the night sky on the patio beside the still glowing barbecue and I had briefly contemplated putting a couple of bullets through the giant speakers; the hunting rifle with its telescopic sights stood in the corner and seemed to be inviting me to use it. Before I could consider taking such drastic action the police came back and confiscated the stereo; in New Zealand they don't wait for a court order to do the sensible thing.

I pulled on my clothes and boots in the darkness, tripping over things in the unfamiliar surroundings. We were staying in my sister Margaret's home in Alexander, in Central Otago, in what the locals called a "sleep-out". This was formerly a garage, away from the house, that had been converted into self-contained sleeping accommodation for guests.

I boiled the kettle and had a quick breakfast, filling the thermos flask with hot water for making tea later on. I assembled a thick sandwich from the remainder of the meat in the small fridge, and packed everything into the rucksack. My moving round had woken Christina; she pulled the duvet tightly over her head and said sarcastically "bring me back a few nuggets". I laughed and slipped out the door into the foggy January morning.

It looked like the makings of a nice day; the fog was lying here in the valley but the hills were clear and picking up the first rays of the rising sun. The big fellow who ran the shearing gang was up and about, throwing equipment into the battered pickup truck. He came across to me as I wiped the heavy dew off the side windows of the Toyota.

"Bloody cops took my bloody stereo," he moaned. He was badly hung over and still slightly drunk.

"I know", I said.

"Did you bloody ring them?" he asked me accusingly.

I looked him straight in the eye. "No", I said, "I was going to, but somebody beat me to it."

He smiled wryly. "Suppose we was asking for it", he said. "Have a good day."

"You too" I said.

I slipped the car in gear and rolled off down the road, picking up speed as I hit the main highway on the outskirts of the town. The morning was brightening at a rapid pace, and the country looked beautiful, with almost nobody out and about. I was eager to get to Matakanui and I gunned the engine on the deserted road, making fast time for the next ten miles.

Close to the racecourse I took the left fork in the road, barely slowing down as I passed through the small settlement here at the junction. A couple of miles farther on I peeled off to the left again, almost losing control of the car when I hit the gravel road to Tinkers. I eased off on the throttle, there was time enough; I had waited a long time to come here, ever since I first heard about the miners and the Undaunted Goldmine, and another few minutes would make no difference.

The miners called this place Tinkers; it has now reverted to its original native name of Matakanui but I will always think of it as Tinkers, with its little dance hall and mud brick houses. A lot of the miners were Irishmen, and they built the small dancehall as soon as they had a few pounds to spare. The little building still stood, with its corrugated iron A-roof and a lean-to at one end for the stage and at the other end for a porch. It looked like any country hall in Ireland, like the one in Killaraght where the Flannerys would have gone to the odd dance on a summer night.

There were not many houses left in Tinkers, just a few old places and no sign of life at this hour of the morning. I pulled the car off the road near the mine and got out, shouldering the rucksack and climbing over the five-bar gate to head across the wasteland towards the hills.

I was walking through the mine workings now, with some old cast-iron sluicing guns and fittings still lying around in the thin grass. The miners would have piped water from a dam up above me in the hills, directing it through successively narrower pipes leading to the sluicing guns, resulting in an extremely high velocity at the nozzle (or the monitor as it was called) of the gun. The ground under my feet was the original subsoil, the so-called "Maori bottom"; the powerful water jets had been used to wash away the gold-bearing strata above this layer. This ground was surprisingly flat; the strata had obviously been level and even along here.

Here and there a "plug" of heavy clay soil stood alone, bypassed by the miners as they washed away the gold-bearing gravel. Some of these were left because they held no valuable sediments; others were untouched because they were the locations of marker pegs for the claims, and it was illegal to interfere with or move these markers. At this stage it was impossible to know the reason why these particular ones had been left. I made my way around these few obstacles, heading all the time for the hills behind the diggings.

From the road, the site didn't seem very big, and I had always assumed that a gold claim was a small patch of ground. Walking through it however, it was clear that this was a huge area; it must have covered a hundred acres at least. The gold bearing stratum, the so-called "paydirt", would have sat on the Maori Bottom, and above it would have been a thicker layer of useless gravel, the so called "overburden". All this would have been washed away and allowed to flow down into the valley into the tailings area, leaving the gold and heavy silt lying on the Maori Bottom. This material would then have been washed down wooden sluices containing iron riffle plates that trapped the heavier gold. As I was walking through the area, I could see clearly the amount of high-pressure water that would have been needed to clear this site; the paydirt and overburden must have been a hundred feet thick in places.

When I got to the back of the workings the hill reared up almost vertically in front of me; they had obviously washed away the gravel until no more remained, and a cliff of clay now blocked my way, impossible to climb. I detoured for a bit in each direction, eventually finding a small landslip that gave me access to the mountain.

I climbed steadily up the steep grassy slope, hauling myself up with the help of the thick grass and the occasional small shrub, and pausing now and then to look back over the mine workings. It was quiet now, and deserted, but this was the place that made their fortunes for the four Flannerys. Here they had dug more gold from the ground than anyone would have thought was possible, from the rich vein of the Undaunted Goldmine. Some of the silty residue that they scooped from the bottom when the gravel had been washed away was almost pure gold. In the years from 1878 to 1912, the Flannerys and their partners took nearly 32,000 ounces of gold from this patch of ground, worth $15,000,000 in today's money. Not bad for a few farm boys from Clooncunny.

A steep climb brought me to the water race; it was dry now, and long grass grew along its length, but I could see it winding its way off into the distance towards Chatto Creek. My heart was racing, and not just from the steep climb; this was the place I had travelled half way around the world to see, and I wasn't disappointed.

I dropped my bag and took a swig from my water bottle, pausing to look back across the valley into the distance. The little settlement of Matakanui was almost invisible below, the old mud-brick houses blending in with the parched landscape. Further on, I saw a puff of smoke from the exhaust of an old yellow mechanical digger, and a second or so later the noise of its engine bursting into life came faintly to me on the still morning air. I knew that a young couple in the locality had begun mining the tailings for gold residues, digging out the gravel into a sluice with an old excavator and finding just enough of the yellow metal to scrape a living from the old gravel wash; gold fever was still alive in this part of the world. The original mining methods had not been very efficient, and it is probable that a lot of gold still remains in the gravel around here.

I could feel the fever myself, a kind of excitement and anticipation that I too could go down to the valley floor and find my fortune with a pan in the bed of a creek. When the gold rush had hit this part of the world, farm workers ran off and left sheep un-sheared and crops rotting in the fields to join in the search for gold. This must have been an amazing place back in the late nineteenth century when the Flannerys built this water race and started to use the high-pressure water jets to blast away tons of gravel from the hillside.

In August 1862 an Irishman called Christopher Reilly and his American partner Horatio Hartley came back to Dunedin from Central Otago and cashed in a sack containing more than a thousand ounces of gold. The ensuing gold rush brought thousands of miners into the area around Cromwell; at the height of the Otago gold rush it was reckoned that the population of these goldfields was well in excess of twenty thousand. It was difficult to believe now, looking down at the deserted valley below me, that this level of activity could have taken place here.

They didn't have an easy life. This place, so hot now in mid summer, has temperatures that plummet in wintertime to almost unbearable levels. Many men died in heavy snowfalls; I recalled seeing one newspaper article of the time that appealed for help in identifying the body of a young man who had fallen into a drunken stupor and frozen to death. Difficulties in getting supplies to this remote region resulted in the miners having a poor diet, and scurvy and other diseases were common.

I picked up the rucksack and set off, along the bed of the now dry race towards the mountains. The channel was dead level underfoot; I could not detect a single low spot or a bit of uneven ground as I walked. It turned around each headland and went in to the mountain, then came back out along the opposite side of each gully to wend its way around that side, staying level all the while. A curious optical illusion made it look as if it was going uphill as it came out of the gullies and downhill as it went in, but as I zigzagged in and out of the hills I could feel no discernable change in the levels.

I must have walked for well more than an hour, as the morning brightened and the sun came up to burn away the fog in the valleys. At about nine o'clock I decided to stop and eat, and to then make my way back the way I had come. It promised to be a scorcher of a day and I was not equipped for a long hike in these lonely hills. I came to a tight bend in the race, where it clung to the steep side of the mountain, and I stopped and sat on a large flat rock just above the channel and dug out my food and the flask.

I sat there for a long time, eating and drinking at my leisure and just soaking up the atmosphere of this fascinating place. I felt very close to the four Flannerys now; I knew that they would probably have sat here just as I did, drinking tea and eating some damper and a bit of mutton or rabbit stew, with their target, the gold claim at Tinkers, now visible in the distance.

In the spot where I stopped the race had been formed by building up a wall of stones and earth on the side of the slope, and lining it with sods and clay. I climbed down to look at it from below; the wall was made from rounded stones bedded in between with earth, in the same way that I had seen field walls and fences made in and around Clooncunny. Here in this far away place, I was looking at the fruits of the hard manual labour of my long-dead relatives, and I found this little detail to be strangely moving. One large stone had become dislodged and had rolled a few yards down the hill; I retrieved it and placed it back in its place in the supporting wall.

The hills in the far distance across from where I now stood formed the outer rim of the Ida Valley, some ten or fifteen miles away. It was here that the Flannerys had gone with their newly acquired wealth, to buy more land than an Irishman could dream of owning. They bought most of the land in the valley, thousands of acres of beautiful fertile land that would feed their families for generations to come. They had no interest in wealth; they just wanted to have some land to call their own and to live in peace. They could have gone back to Ireland and lived as rich men, but that was never part of the plan.

There are some small clues that tell us what drove these men on to surmount almost impossible odds and bring in this gold claim. They built a house in the Ida Valley, a modest place suitable for a strong farmer, but not ostentatious or vulgar. The name on the house today is still the same, when I drove through the valley a few days later along the highway that is called Flannery Road I could see the nameplate still on the gateposts. They called the house Coolavin, the same as the big house back in Ireland where the McDermotts lived with all their comforts in the middle of all the poverty of their peasant neighbours. The second house they built was called "Clooncunny" after their much-loved home village, a place they would never see again.

The sun was rising now, and the day was getting hotter, so I picked up my bag and set off back the way I had come. The dew was drying off the arid grass and I could feel the sun beating down on my head; there is an intensity about the sun in summer in Central Otago that can burn you black in a very short time. I made good time on the return leg, cutting off from the little canal at the near end of the diggings and heading back along the flat bottom to the car. I turned once to look back up the mountain at the race; I could barely see the level horizontal line that marked its path, and I knew that it would soon disappear from my view, merging into the arid grassy brown hillside. I said goodbye to the four Flannerys and headed for the car.

The journey back took me a lot longer; I was driving slowly, my head full of all I had seen. At last I had been able to visit the place I had imagined for so long. It was good to walk in the footsteps of men I greatly admired, and to see the little details of what they had done when they left Ireland to find a new life in this place.

I found a parking place outside the library, and I walked in to see if I could find out more. I was conscious that my boots were leaving dirt on the shining floor, but the sprightly woman behind the counter had a smile that was warm and welcoming. "What can I get for you today?" she asked, and she seemed to be genuinely anxious to help.

"I'm looking for some information on the mines, the goldmines around Tinkers," I said.

"Any mine in particular?" she asked.

I told her about the four Flannery's and the water race and the Undaunted Mine, and she smiled again.

"The famous Flannerys" she said, "Oh, I know all about them, they were fine people."

She went to a shelf behind the desk and pulled out a heavy encyclopaedia from a set of four or five volumes. Giving it a practiced wipe with a duster she opened it near the middle, turning a few pages quickly until she found what she wanted. She smiled triumphantly and pointed at the page, twirling the big book around on the polished counter top so that it faced me. "There you are", she said, jabbing a finger at an article that was headed "Matakanui". "There", she said, "I knew it was there, the famous Flannerys, indeed."

I took the heavy volume back to one of the tables and read the article over and over. The book had been published in 1905, shortly after the mine had been listed on the London Stock Exchange. I turned the page and saw an etching of an old photograph, with the massive jets of water from the sluicing guns cutting away at the gravel, and the tiny black-waistcoated figures of the miners down below on the bottom.

I brought the book back to the smiling lady at the desk, and she offered to photocopy the pages for me. She turned away and fussed around the photocopier, waiting for it to warm up. "You're not from around here", she said, but by the tone of her voice it was meant as a polite question.

I was looking out the window to the square, where a huge cat stretched lazily on the window ledge in the hot sun. "I'm from Ireland", I said.

"I kinda thought that", she said. "Are you one of the Flannerys by any chance?"

I was staring out past the square, where the sheep-shearing boss chugged down the street away from the beer shop in his battered pickup. The crew would have a massive hangover, and it was time for their tea break. "I'm sorry, I said, "My mind was on something else".

"Are you one of the Flannery clan?" she asked.

I hesitated for a moment, and the cat jumped down from the window ledge and strolled off stiff-legged to look for some shade.

"Yes" I said, "You could say that, right enough".

"Imagine that!" she said. "That'll be fifty cents for the copies."

The Aurelia Trust

All author royalties and publisher's profits from this edition of *Following in the Footsteps of the Four Famous Flannerys* go to the Aurelia Trust, an Irish non-government voluntary organisation working in Central and Eastern Europe. The trust can be contacted at 37 North Street, Skibbereen, County Cork, Ireland.

The trust's objectives include the prevention of the abandonment and institutionalisation of children by supporting vulnerable families and providing alternative care such as fostering and adoption. It seeks to improve the lives of institutionalised children by providing staff training and ensuring that children are receiving adequate care and attention, in order that they can live as normal a life as possible within the confines of an institution. It challenges childcare policy, practice and legislation where appropriate in order to promote a child and family-centred care system.

In buying this book, you have helped the trust with its work. If you want to be of further assistance, donations and bequests are welcome to:

Aurelia Trust
c/o Bank of Ireland, Skibbereen, County Cork.
Sort Code 90-29-52
Account Number 78722361

www.fourflannerys.com